"ACE" ANY

TEST

FIFTH EDITION

"ACE" ANY
TEST

FIFTH EDITION

by RON FRY

THOMSON
━━━━━━━✦━━━━━━━ ™
DELMAR LEARNING

Australia Canada Mexico Singapore Spain United Kingdom United States

THOMSON

DELMAR LEARNING

"Ace" Any Test, Fifth Edition
Ron Fry

Vice President,
Career Education SBU:
Dawn Gerrain

Director of Editorial:
Sherry Gomoll

Acquisitions Editor:
Martine Edwards

Developmental Editor:
Shelley Esposito

Editorial Assistant:
Paul Carmon

Director of Production:
Wendy A. Troeger

Production Editor:
Joy Kocsis

Director of Marketing:
Wendy E. Mapstone

Cover Design:
Joseph Villanova

Composition:
TIPS Technical
Publishing, Inc.

Cover Image:
© Getty Images

For permission to use material from this
text or product, submit a request online
at http://www.thomsonrights.com

Any additional questions about permis-
sions can be submitted by email to
thomsonrights@thomson.com

Library of Congress Cataloging-in-
Publication Data

Fry, Ronald W.
   "Ace" any test / Ron Fry.--5th ed.
      p.cm.-- (Ron Fry's how to study program)
   Includes index.
   ISBN 1-4018-8912-3

1. Examinations--United States--Study
guides. 2. Test-taking skills--United States.
I. Title.

LB3060.57.F79 2005
371.26--dc22

2004008796

NOTICE TO THE READER

Contents

There Will Be *a Quiz on This*

I n case you feel there aren't enough tests already, the No Child Left Behind Act of 2001 mandated annual tests for math and reading proficiency for grades three through eight. Starting in the fall of 2007, children in these grades will also be tested in science.

Since two-thirds of students are not proficient readers when they leave school, and I suspect a majority probably couldn't balance a checkbook, it's hard to argue that something has to be done. But more tests? Just what you need, right?

The book you are holding in your hand is now in its fourth edition, and has been helping students and parents (and even teachers) for 15 years. (The other books in my **How to Study Program—How to Study** itself, **Get Organized, Improve Your Memory, Improve Your Reading**, and **Improve Your Writing**—are also now available in new editions.)

Thank you for making these books so successful.

I cannot take very much credit for their longevity. Unfortunately, the state of affairs that existed in 1988, when I wrote the first edition of **How to Study**, has not improved—teachers are still underpaid, students are still undertaught, schools are still underfunded, and study skills are still underutilized, the No Child Left Behind Act notwithstanding. As a result, my **How to Study Program** is, for many of you, parents and students alike, the only source of information about the vital skills needed to succeed both in school and in life.

SO WHO ARE YOU?

A number of you are students, not just the high school students I always thought were my readers, but also college students and *junior* high school students.

Many of you reading this are adults. Some of you are returning to school, and some of you are long out of school, but if you can learn *now* the study skills your teachers never taught you, you will do better in your careers.

All too many of you are parents with the same lament: "How do I get Jill to do better in school? She just doesn't test well."

If you're a high school student, you should be particularly comfortable with both the language and format of this book—its relatively short sentences and paragraphs, occasionally humorous (hopefully) headings and sub-headings, and a reasonable but certainly not outrageous vocabulary. I wrote it with you in mind!

If you're a junior high school student, you are trying to learn how to study at *precisely* the right time. If you're serious enough about studying to be reading this book, I doubt you'll have trouble with the concepts or the language.

If you're a "traditional" college student, who went right on to college from high school, how'd you manage that leap without mastering test-taking techniques? Well, here you are, facing more and tougher tests than ever before.

If you're the parent of a student of any age, your child's school is probably doing little if anything to teach him how to study. Which means he is not learning how to *learn*. And *that* means he is not learning how to *succeed*.

Should the schools be accomplishing that? Absolutely. After all, we spend more than $300 billion on elementary and secondary education in this country. We ought to be getting more for that money than a diploma, some football cheers, and a rotten entry-level job market.

WHAT CAN PARENTS DO?

Okay, here they are, the rules for parents of students of any age:

1. **Set up a homework area**. Free of distraction, well lit, with all necessary supplies handy.

2. **Set up a homework routine**. When and where it gets done. Studies have clearly shown that students who establish a regular routine are better organized and, as a result, more successful.

3. **Set homework priorities**. Actually, just make the point that homework *is* the priority—before a date, before TV, before going out to play, whatever.

4. **Make reading a habit**—for them, certainly, but also for yourselves. Kids will inevitably do what you *do*, not what you *say* (even if you say *not* to do what you *do*).

5. **Turn off the TV.** Or at the very least, severely limit when and how much TV watching is appropriate. This may be the toughest suggestion to enforce. I know. I'm the parent of a teenager.

6. **Talk to the teachers.** Find out what your kids are supposed to be learning. If you don't know the books they're supposed to be reading, what's expected of them in class, and how much homework they should be scheduling, you can't really give them the help they need.

7. **Encourage and motivate**, but don't nag them to do their homework. It doesn't work. The more you insist, the quicker they will tune you out.

8. **Supervise their work**, but don't fall into the trap of doing their homework. Checking (i.e., proofreading) a paper, for example, is a positive way to help your child in school. But if you simply put in corrections without your child learning from her mistakes, you're not helping her at all...except in the belief that she is not responsible for her own work.

9. **Praise them when they succeed**, but don't over-praise them for mediocre work. Kids know when you're being insincere and, again, will quickly tune you out.

10. **Convince them of reality**. (This is for older students.) Okay, I'll admit it's almost as much of a stretch as turning off the TV, but learning and believing that the real world will not care about their grades, but will measure them by what they know and what they can do, is a lesson that will save many tears (probably yours). It's probably never too early to (carefully) let your boy or girl genius get the message that life is not fair.

11. **If you can afford it, get your kid(s) a computer** and all the software they can handle. There really is no avoiding it: Your kids, whatever their ages, absolutely must be computer savvy in order to survive in and after school.

12. **Turn off the TV already!**

13. **Get wired.** The Internet is the greatest invention of our age and an unbelievable tool for students of any age. It is impossible for a college student to succeed without the ability to surf the Web, and nearly impossible for younger students. They've got to be connected.

14. **But turn off IM (Instant Messaging) while doing homework.** They will attempt to convince you that they can write a term paper, do their geometry homework, and IM their friends at the same time. Parents who believe this have also been persuaded that the best study area is in front of the TV.

DOS AND DON'TS ABOUT TESTS AND TESTING

1. Don't get overanxious about your child's test scores. Too much emphasis solely on grades can upset a child, especially one already chafing under too much pressure.

2. Children who are afraid of failing are more likely to make mistakes on tests. Help them feel confident about everything they do.

3. Don't judge your child by a single test score, no matter how important the test. No test is a perfect

measure of what a child can do or what she has actually learned.

4. Talk to your child's teacher as often as possible. Her assessment will be a far better measure of how your child is doing than any test, or even any series of tests.

5. Make sure your child attends school regularly. You can't do well on tests if you are rarely in class.

6. Make sure your child gets enough sleep, especially before a big test. Tired eyes lead to tired grades.

7. Review test results with your child and show them what they can learn from a graded exam paper. This is especially crucial in math and the sciences, where a new concept builds upon the previous ones.

8. Look at the wrong answers. Find out why she answered as she did. This will identify times when your child knew the right answer but didn't fully understand the question.

9. Read and discuss any teacher comments on the test, especially if your child received a poor grade.

THE IMPORTANCE OF YOUR INVOLVEMENT

Don't underestimate the importance of *your* commitment to your child's success: Your involvement in your child's education is absolutely essential to her eventual success. The results of every study done in the last two decades about what affects a child's success in school clearly demonstrate that only one factor *overwhelmingly* affects it, every time: parental involvement—not the size of the school, the money spent per pupil, the number of language labs, how many of the students go on to college, how many great (or lousy) teachers there are. All factors, yes. *But none as significant as the effect you can have.*

You can help tremendously, *even if you were not a great student, even if you never learned great study skills.*

IF YOU'RE A NONTRADITIONAL STUDENT

If you're going back to high school, college, or graduate school at age 25, 45, 65, or 85—you probably need the help my books offer more than anyone! Why? Because the longer you've been out of school, the more likely it is that you don't remember what you've forgotten. And you've probably forgotten what you're supposed to remember! As much as I emphasize that it's rarely too early to learn good study habits, I must also emphasize that it's never too late.

If you're returning to school and attempting to carry even a partial load of courses while simultaneously holding down a job, raising a family, or both, there are some particular problems you face that you probably didn't the first time you were in school.

Time and money pressures. Let's face it: When all you had to worry about was going to school, it simply *had* to be easier than going to school, raising a family, and working for a living simultaneously. (And it was!)

Self-imposed fears of inadequacy. You may convince yourself that you're "out of practice" with all this school stuff. You don't even remember what to do with a highlighter! While some of this fear is valid, most is not. The valid part is that you're returning to an academic atmosphere, one you may not have even visited for a decade or two. I suspect what many of you are really afraid of is that the skills you need to succeed in school are rusty.

Maybe you're worried because you didn't exactly light up the academic power plant the first time around. Well, neither did Edison or Einstein or a host of other relatively successful people. Concentrate on how much *more* qualified you are for school *now* than you were *then!*

Feeling you're "out of your element." This is a slightly different fear, the fear that you just don't fit in any more. After all, you're not 18 again. But then, neither are fully half the college students on campus today. That's right: More than 50 percent of all college students are older than 25. The reality is, you'll probably feel more in your element now than you did the first time around!

You'll see teachers differently. True. So what? At worst, you'll consider teachers your equals. At best, you'll consider them younger and not necessarily as successful or experienced as you are. In either event, you probably won't be quite as ready to treat your college professors as if they were visiting from Olympus.

There *are* differences in academic life. It's slower than the "real" world, and you may well be moving significantly faster than its normal pace. When you were 18, an afternoon without classes meant a game of Frisbee. Now it might mean catching up on a week's worth of errands, cooking (and freezing) a week's worth of dinners, and/or writing four reports due last week. Despite your own hectic schedule, do not expect campus life to accelerate in response. You will have to get used to people and systems with far less interest in speed.

SOME RANDOM THOUGHTS ABOUT LEARNING

Learning shouldn't be painful and certainly doesn't have to be boring, though it's far too often both. However, it's not necessarily going to be wonderful and painless, either. Sometimes you actually have to work hard to figure something out or get a project done. That *is* reality.

It's also reality that everything isn't readily apparent or easily understandable. Confusion reigns. Tell yourself that's okay and learn how to get past it. Heck, if you actually think you're supposed to understand everything you read the first time through, you're kidding yourself. Learning something slowly doesn't mean there's something wrong with you. It may be a subject that virtually everybody learns slowly. Or a poorly written textbook that is to blame. A good student just takes his time, follows whatever steps apply, and remains confident that the lightbulb of understanding will eventually click on.

Parents often ask me, "How can I motivate my teenager?" My initial response is usually to smile and say, "If I knew the answer to that question, I would have retired very wealthy quite some time ago." However, I think there *is* an answer, but it's not something *parents* can do—it's something you, the student, have to decide: Are you going to spend the school day interested and alert or bored and resentful?

It's really that simple. Since you have to go to school anyway, why not develop the attitude that you might as well be active and learn as much as possible instead of being miserable? The difference between a C and an A or B for many students is, I firmly believe, merely a matter of wanting to do better. As I constantly stress in radio and TV interviews, inevitably you will leave school. And very quickly, you'll discover all everyone really cares about is what you know and what you can do. Grades won't count anymore; neither will tests. So you can learn it all now or regret it later.

How many times have you said to yourself, "I don't know why I'm bothering trying to learn this calculus, algebra, geometry, physics, chemistry, history, whatever. I'll *never* use this again!"? Unless you've just patented some great new fortune-telling device, you have *no clue* what you're going to need to know tomorrow or next week, let alone next year or in a decade.

I've been amazed in my own life how things I did with no specific purpose in mind (except probably to earn money or meet a girl) turned out years later to be not just invaluable to my life or career, but essential. How was I to know when I took German as my language elective in high school that the most important international trade show in book publishing was in Frankfurt, Germany? Or that the basic skills I learned one year working for an accountant (while I was writing my first book) would become essential when I later started four companies? Or how important basic math skills would be in selling and negotiating over the years? (Okay, I'll admit it: I haven't used a differential equation in 20 years, but, hey, you never know!)

So learn it *all*. And don't be surprised if the subject you'd vote "Least likely to ever be useful" winds up being the key to *your* fame and fortune.

There Aren't Many Study Rules

Though I immodestly maintain that my **How to Study Program** is the most helpful to the most people, there are certainly plenty of other purported study books out there. Inevitably, these other books promote the authors' "system," which usually means what *they* did to get through school. This "system," whether basic and traditional or wildly quirky, may or may not work for you. So what do you do if "their" way of taking notes makes no sense to you? Or you master their highfalutin' "Super Student Study Symbols" and still get Cs?

There are very few "rights" and "wrongs" out there in the study world. There's certainly no single "right" way to attack a multiple choice test or take notes. So don't get fooled into thinking there *is*, especially if what you're doing seems to be working for you.

Needless to say, don't read *my* books looking for that single, inestimable system of "rules" that works for everyone. You won't find it, 'cause there's no such bird. You *will* find a plethora of techniques, tips, tricks, gimmicks, and what-have-you, some or all of which may work for you, some of which won't. Pick and choose, change and adapt, figure out what works for you. Because *you* are the one responsible for creating *your* study system, *not me.*

I've used the phrase "Study smarter, not harder" as a sort of catch phrase in promotion and publicity for the **How to Study Program** for nearly two decades. So what does it mean to you? Does it mean I guarantee you'll spend less time studying? Or that the least amount of time is best? Or that studying isn't ever supposed to be hard?

Hardly. It does mean that studying inefficiently is wasting time that could be spent doing other (okay, probably more *fun*) things and that getting your studying done as quickly and efficiently as possible is a realistic, worthy, and *attainable* goal. I'm no stranger to hard work, but I'm not a monastic dropout who thrives on self-flagellation. I try not to work harder than I have to!

IT'S A HARD-WIRED WORLD

In 1988, when I wrote the first edition of **How to Study**, I composed it, formatted it, and printed it on (gasp) a personal computer. Most people did *not* have a computer, yet alone a neighborhood network and DSL, or surf the Web (whatever that was), or chat online, or Instant Message their friends, or...you get the point.

In case you've been living in a cave that Bill Gates forgot to wire, those days are very dead and gone. And you should cheer, even if you aren't sure what DOS was (is? could be?). Because the spread of the personal computer and, even more important, the Internet, has taken studying from the Dark Ages to the Info Age in merely a decade.

As a result, you will find all of my books assume you have a computer and know how to use it—for note taking, reading, writing papers, researching, and much more. There are many tasks that may be harder on a computer—and I'll point them out—but don't believe for a second that a computer won't help you tremendously, whatever your age, whatever your grades.

As for the Internet, it has absolutely revolutionized research. Whether you're writing a paper, putting together a reading list, studying for the SAT, or just trying to organize your life, it has become a more valuable tool than the greatest library in the world. Heck, it *is* the greatest library in the world...and more. So if you are not Internet savvy (yes, I'm talking to the parents out there, couldn't you tell?), admit you're a dummy, get a book (over the Internet, of course), and get wired. You'll be missing far too much—and be studying far harder—without it.

HE/SHE, WOMYN, (S)HE

Before we get on with all the tips and techniques necessary to make tests quake when they see you coming, let me make two important points about all of my study books.

First, I believe in gender equality, but I find constructions such as "he and she," "s/he," "womyn," and other such stretches to be sometimes painfully awkward. I have therefore attempted to sprinkle pronouns of both genders throughout the text.

Second, you will find that many similar pieces of advice, examples, lists, terms, phrases, and sections appear in several of my books. Certainly **How to Study**, which is an overview of all the study skills, necessarily contains, though in summarized form, some of each of the other five books.

The repetition is unavoidable. While I urge everyone to read all the books in the series, but especially **How to Study**, they *are* six individual books. And many people buy only one of them. Consequently, I must include in each book the pertinent material *for that topic*, even if that material is repeated in another book.

That said, I can guarantee that the nearly 1,000 pages of my **How to Study Program** contain the most wide-ranging, comprehensive, and complete system of studying ever published. I have attempted to create a system that is usable, useful, practical, and learnable. One that *you* can use—whatever your age, whatever your level of achievement, whatever your IQ—to start doing better in school, in work, and in life *immediately*.

Good luck.

Ron Fry

Overcome
Your Fear

> *"WE HAVE NOTHING TO FEAR BUT FEAR ITSELF."*
> *—FRANKLIN DELANO ROOSEVELT*

F DR was almost right. The only thing you may have to fear is fear itself. But, frankly, you don't have to. You just have to conquer it or beat it into submission so you can get on with your life—and your biology exam.

Let's spend a few minutes talking about why tests scare people. Then I'll help you learn how to spend your time studying instead of wasting it on anxiety attacks.

THE SOUND OF TWO KNEES KNOCKING

I saw a documentary on a famous singer some years ago. The camera followed her as she went to rehearsal, got made up, and talked to her manager.

The scene I remember most was as she waited back-stage to be announced—she looked nervous, horrified, petrified, regretful that she'd ever entered show business, and extremely vulnerable.

But when the announcer called her name and the roar of applause began, she walked with a determined gait to the stage, smiled, took the microphone, and looked anything but frightened. Her famous voice filled the auditorium, and the audience went wild. If she was petrified and still passed the test, why shouldn't you?

Why are we so afraid, especially of tests? Because we don't want to fail. We realize that, within the next 30 or 60 minutes, a percentage of our grade will be determined by what we write on a piece of paper or which box we fill in with our No. 2 pencil. And the bigger the test, the greater the anxiety.

So WHAT ARE *YOU* AFRAID OF?

What does it mean when someone proclaims they don't "test well?" For many, it really means they don't *study* well (or, at the very least, prepare well). For others, it could mean they are easily distracted, unprepared for the type of test they are confronting, or simply unprepared mentally to take *any* test.

We all recognize the competitive nature of tests. Some of us rise to the occasion when facing such a challenge. Others are thrown off balance by the pressure. Both reactions probably have little to do with one's level of knowledge, relative intelligence, or amount of preparation. The smartest students in your class may be the ones most afraid of tests.

Sometimes, it's not fear of failure, but fear of *success*. You think to yourself, "If I do well on this exam, my parents will expect me to do well on the next exam, and the teacher will think I'm going to do well every day!"

Please. Look at it this way: You'll have to deal with some sort of pressure every day of your life. So you might as well learn to handle the *good* kind ("Way to go, genius, keep up the good work!") rather than face the other ("I just don't understand why Tim does so poorly in school. He just doesn't apply himself").

She's done *already?*

Another reason for failure? Some people can't deal with competition. All they can think about is what Abby is doing. Look at her! She's sitting there, filling in one answer after another—and you know they're all correct!

Who cares about Abby? I sure wouldn't. Only one person in that room should be concerned with Abby and her performance. That's right. Just as only one person should be concerned with your performance. Make it all a game: Compete with yourself. See if you can't beat your previous test scores. That's positive competition!

My then-11-year-old daughter Lindsay clarified this point when she ran the 100-yard dash for her fifth-grade track team. Despite the fact she was the second fastest of nearly 50 girls, she cried at the end of the race because she hadn't finished *first*. It must be her mother's genes.

You don't have to join their club

Some people thrive on their own misery and are jealous if you don't feed on it, too. They want to suck you into their gloom, whether you really know or care what's happening.

These Anxiety Professionals are the people to avoid when you're preparing for an exam. "Oh, I'll never learn all this stuff!" they cry. You might not win points with Ms. Manners if you say, "If you'd shut up and study, you might!" But you *can* have the pleasure of *thinking* it—on your way to a quiet place to study alone.

Watch out for those "friends" who call you the night before the exam to wail, "I just found out we have to know Chapter 12!" Don't fall into their trap. Instead of dialing 911, calmly remind them that the printed sheet the professor passed out two weeks ago clearly says that the test will cover Chapters 6 through 11. Then hang up, get on with your life, and let them wring their hands all the way to the bottom of the grading sheet. (Of course, if you don't bother to check what's going to be on the test, a call like this will panic you...and waste your time.)

Think of this fraction: one over one million. Your life is the big number. Your next test is the little number. All the "ones" in your life add up to the one million; they are important, but all by themselves, they can't compare to the Giant Economy Number of Life. Write "1/1,000,000" at the top of your next test to remind yourself of that. It's a sure way to obliterate a bunch of stomach butterflies.

"EXTRA" TESTS GIVE EXTRA HELP

If you want to practice the many recommendations you're going to get in this book, including what I'm sharing with you in this important first chapter, take a few "extra" tests just to give yourself some practice. This will also help you overcome unacceptable levels of test anxiety.

Get permission from your teachers to retake some old tests to practice test-taking techniques and exorcise the High-Anxiety Demon. Many teachers' tests (as well as lecture notes and sample papers) are available in the school's library. And take a couple of the standardized tests your counseling office probably has, too, since the fill-in-the-box answer sheets and questions in printed form have their own set of rules.

A LITTLE PERSPECTIVE, PLEASE

The more pressure you put on yourself—the larger you allow a test (and, of course, your hoped-for good scores) to loom in your own mind—the less you are helping yourself. Of course, the bigger the test really *is*, the *harder* it is to avoid reminding yourself of its importance.

No matter how important a test really may be to your career—and your scores on some can have a major effect on where you go to college, whether you go on to graduate school, whether you get the job you want—it is just as important to *de-emphasize* that test's importance in your mind. This should have no effect on your preparation—you should still study as if your life depended on a superior score. It might!

A friend of mine signed up to take the Law School Admission Test (LSAT), not just once, but twice. The first time, he did "okay, not great." By the time the second date rolled around, he had come to his senses and decided not to become a lawyer. But since he had already paid for the thing, he took the LSAT again anyway. Are you already ahead of me? That's right—a 15 percent improvement with no studying. Does that tell you something about trying to downplay all this self-inflicted pressure?

Keeping the whole experience in perspective might also help: Twenty years from now, nobody will remember, or care, what you scored on any test—no matter how life-threatening or life-determining you feel that test is now.

Don't underestimate positive thinking: Thoughts can become self-fulfilling prophecies. If you tell yourself often enough, "Be careful, you'll fall over that step," you probably will. If you tell yourself often enough, "I'm going to fail this test," you just might. Likewise, keep convincing yourself that you are as prepared as anyone and are going to "ace" the sucker, and you're already ahead of the game.

How to lower your AQ (Anxiety Quotient)

When a test is looming, knowing the answers to as many of these questions as possible will help reduce your anxiety:

1. What material will the exam cover?
2. How many total points are possible?
3. What will this exam count for?
4. How much time will I have to take the exam?
5. Where will the exam be held?
6. What kinds of questions will be on the exam (matching, multiple choice, essay, true/false, and so forth)?
7. How many of each type of question will be on the exam?
8. How many points will be assigned to each question?
9. Will certain sections of the test count more than others?
10. Will it be an open-book exam?
11. What can I take in with me? Calculator? Candy bar? Other material crucial to my success?
12. Will I be penalized for wrong answers?

TAKE A HIKE, BUDDY

Finally, to shake off pretest anxiety, take a walk, or a vigorous swim. In the days before an exam, no matter how "big" it is, don't study too hard or too much, or you'll walk into the exam with a fried brain.

Please don't think that advice loses its power at the classroom door. Scheduling breaks during tests has the same effect. During a one-hour test, you may not have time to go out for a stroll. But during a two- or three-hour final, there's no reason you should not schedule one, two, or even more breaks on a periodic basis—whenever you feel you need them most. Such timeouts can consist of a bathroom stop, a quick walk up and down the hall, or just a minute of relaxation in your seat before you continue the test.

No matter what the time limits or pressures, don't feel you cannot afford such a brief respite. You may need it *most* when you're convinced you can least afford it, just as those who most need time-management techniques "Just don't have the time" to learn them.

RELAX, DARN IT!

If your mind is a jumble of facts and figures, names and dates, you may find it difficult to zero in on the specific details you need to recall, even if you know all the material backwards and forwards. The adrenaline rushing through your system may make "instant retrieval" seem impossible.

The simplest relaxation technique is deep breathing. Just lean back in your chair, relax your muscles, and take three very deep breaths (count to 10 while you hold each one). For many of you, that's the only relaxation technique you'll ever need.

There are a variety of meditation techniques that may also work for you. Each is based upon a similar principle—focusing your mind on one thing to the exclusion of everything else. While you're concentrating on the object of your meditation (even if the object is nothing, a nonsense word, or a spot on the wall,) your mind can't be thinking about anything else, which allows it to slow down a bit.

But don't go into a trance yet—we have a lot more ground to cover.

Creating the Time to Study

"WORK EXPANDS SO AS TO FILL THE TIME AVAILABLE FOR ITS COMPLETION."
—CYRIL PARKINSON, PARKINSON'S LAW

"I RECOMMEND THAT YOU LEARN TO TAKE CARE OF THE MINUTES, FOR THE HOURS WILL TAKE CARE OF THEMSELVES."
—LORD CHESTERFIELD

● ● ●

We all have problems with time. We can't slow it down, speed it up, or save it up—all we can do is decide how we're going to spend it. We invariably need more of it...and don't know where to find it. Then we wonder where the heck it all went.

But time isn't really the problem. We all get the same 24 hours. The problem is that most of us have never been taught how to manage our time...or why we should even try. Our parents never sat us down to give us a little "facts of time" talk, and time-management skills aren't part of most academic curricula.

Not knowing how to effectively manage our time, we let it continue to dribble through our fingers—taking things as they come and doing what we feel like doing, without schedule or plan. What the heck, it worked when we were kids. It was easy to live from day to day and never really worry about where our time went.

In fact, sometimes there seemed to be too *much* time—too many *hours* before school was over...too many *days* before summer vacation...too many *weeks* before birthdays...too many *years* before we could be on our own.

There comes a point—too soon, perhaps—when the take-every-day-as-it-comes approach just doesn't work. For most of us, it hits in high school. (If you're in high school and don't know what I'm talking about, don't worry—you'll find out in college.) Why? Because that's when we begin to establish goals that are important to *us*, not just to our parents.

To achieve our goals, we must commit ourselves to the many and varied steps it takes to get there. We must plan. We must *manage* our time.

Whether you're a high school student just starting to feel frazzled, a college student juggling five classes and a part-time job, or a parent working, attending classes, and raising a family, a simple, easy-to-follow time-management system is crucial to your success. Despite your natural tendency to proclaim that you just don't have the *time* to spend scheduling, listing, and recording, it's actually the best way to give yourself *more* time.

Between now and next Tuesday, whether you are preparing to play in the state basketball tournament, writing a paper about the Knights Templar, or holding down three jobs (or, heaven help you, all of the above), you have exactly the same amount of time as the rest of us. It's what you *do* with that time that makes the difference.

How are you going to get from here to there? Are you just going to go crashing along, like an elephant trampling down banana trees, or are you going to reach your goals by following a plan? Good. That's the right answer. You just passed *another* test.

YOU'RE SPENDING THREE HOURS A DAY RESTING?

The first step to overhauling your current routine is to identify that routine, in detail. My suggestion is to chart, in 15-minute increments, how you spend every minute of every day, right now. While keeping track of your activities for a day or two might be sufficient for some of you, I recommend you chart them for an entire week, including the weekend.

You may also use the chart on p. 24 to assess how much time you actually have available for studying. If it's clearly not enough, then you'd better reassess how much time you're spending in each of the other areas. You may have to cut your part-time work hours, quit a club, even change your schedule to reduce your commute. Of course, if you're spending two hours a day on "grooming" or six hours eating, the solution may be a little more obvious.

Like many people, you probably have huge pockets of time that seemingly disappear, but are devoted to things like "resting" after you wake up, putting on makeup and shaving, reading the paper, waiting for transportation, or driving to and from school or work. Could you use an extra hour or two a day, either for studying or for fun? Make better use of such "dead" time and you may well find the time you need.

Learn how to do multiple tasks at the same time. Listen to a book on tape while you're working around the house; practice vocabulary or math drills while you're driving; have your kids, parents, or roommates quiz you for an upcoming test while you're doing the dishes, vacuuming, or dusting. And *always* carry your calendar, note-book(s), pens, and a textbook with you. You'll be surprised how much reading or studying you can do while in line at the bank, in the library, at the supermarket, or riding on a bus or train.

The more willing you are to transform "dead" time into study time, the more ways you'll invent to do so.

Focus = efficiency

How often have you made a "to-do" list and then either forgotten it, lost it, or ignored it? To-do lists have incredible merits, but they're not much good if you don't use them. You can't effectively deal with *today's* priorities if you still have to contend with yesterday's...or last week's!

Let's run through the composition and execution of a to-do list for a shopping expedition as an example. Here's what I do when I am making up a list of errands:

First, after writing down where I have to go, I turn the paper over and make individual lists of items for each stopping place. So after entering "Smith's Drugstore" on my to-do list, I write my shopping list—shaving cream, bubble gum, newspaper, hair spray, and prescription—on the back.

By separating the *where* from the *what*, I am able to focus on getting from the post office to the drug store to the hardware store, without trying to separate the stamps from the toothpaste and tool kit.

I do one more thing on my shopping list: If I need to take anything with me (return a video, drop off my dry cleaning, take an article to be photocopied), I place a "T" (meaning "take") with a circle around it beside the place for which I need the "T" item. That way, I don't get to Smith's only to discover that I forgot to bring the prescription form. (If convenient, put all the "T" items, along with the list, beside the door so you won't have to search for them when it's time to leave.)

Where Does Your Time Go?

	Hrs./Day	Days/Wk	Hrs./Wk
Meals (including prep and clean up)	_____	7	_____
Sleeping (including naps)	_____	7	_____
Grooming	_____	7	_____
Commuting	_____	5?	_____
Errands	_____	7	_____
Extracurricular activities	_____	_____	_____
Part- or full-time job	_____	_____	_____
In class	_____	_____	_____
Entertainment*	_____	_____	_____

*Hanging with friends, going out, watching TV, reading for pleasure, etc

Fill in the first column, multiply by the second, then total the third column. There are 168 hours in a week (24 x 7). How many do you currently have left for studying? Note: Any answer that contains a minus is a *bad* sign.

SHOPPING FOR GOOD GRADES

Think of the time between now and your next exam as your shopping trip. You want to use this time most effectively so that you: (1) don't forget anything, (2) work efficiently (save time), (3) arrange your studying so it's done as easily as possible, and (4) concentrate on the important details, not on *all* the details (big difference!).

You need to assess what you *must* do, what you *should* do and what you *want* to do. Let's refer to them as our H, M, and L priorities.

The H ("high") priorities are those things we *must* do between now and the next test.

The M ("medium") priorities are those things we *should* do, but we could conceivably postpone them without being jailed or written out of anyone's will.

The L ("low") priorities are things we want to do, but they are *expendable*, at least until you have finished taking this next exam. (Feel free to use A, B, C or 1, 2, 3 or any other system for prioritizing your tasks, but don't utilize fewer than three levels of importance.)

IT'S ALL RIGHT TO SLEEP

An "H" is sleeping, eating, and attending class—especially the class in question. You simply can't ignore these priorities.

An "M" is getting your car's oil changed or taking your cat to the vet for a checkup. Important, but unless the car's dipstick shows that it has no oil or the cat is so sick it's trying to dial the vet's number itself, these tasks can be delayed for a day or more.

An "L" is going to the Kurosawa Film Festival or partying with friends.

I've included two key tools from the new edition of **Get Organized** in this book as well. The first—the Long-Term Calendar—will help you sort out and manage the big picture. The second—the Daily Calendar—separates the semester into seven day periods. These are the only two forms most of you will need to manage your time.

Let's talk about the long-term calendar, a sample of which is on p. 28, and a blank you can photocopy on p. 29. Simply put, this is a series of monthly calendars with all the important events listed on them. Sounds pretty simple. Actually, it is. Even if you've only got six weeks left in the semester, go ahead and fill out one of these.

Don't just list school-related items ("Biology semester exam, 9 a.m." on May 3); put down the "H" items from the rest of your life, too ("Trip to Chicago" on March 22).

One very good reason for listing all the social/personal/nonacademic items is for you to determine which of them should *remain* in the "H" category. For example, if you discover that your Chicago trip is scheduled for the weekend before your French midterm, you'd better cry *"Sacre bleu!"* and move it (now an "L") to another weekend.

GET THE PICTURE?

One of the most important reasons for *writing down everything* that is coming up is to see that big picture. Once you've filled in all the due dates of term papers, unit tests, midterms, finals, project reports, and so forth, take a good look at the results.

Are there a bunch of deadlines in the same week or even on the same day? During finals and midterms, of course, this really can't be helped—they're often scheduled in a single week or less.

Perhaps you can do something about some of the other deadlines. If you have a French test covering three units on the same day that you have to turn in a paper on "The Influence of the Beatles on British Foreign Policy" and a status report on your gerbil project for sociology, take the plunge and decide that you will get the paper and the project report done early so that you can devote the time just prior to that day to studying for your French test.

You can't make decisions like that, however, if you are unable to sit back and get an overall view. Seeing everything that is coming up "at a glance" will help you decide what is really an "H" and what is not. It need not cut into your social life, but it may mean that you have to occasionally rearrange some things or decline invitations that conflict with important deadlines.

But you can frolic on the nights and weekends that are far enough away from your "H" priorities. When personal "H" events come up (you really can't miss your sister's wedding, no matter how much the gerbils need you), your long-term calendar will give you enough warning so your schoolwork needn't suffer.

I SHOULD HAVE PLANNED BETTER

Once you have a grasp of your obligations for the full term, concentrate on the week at hand and fill out your daily calendar. (See the samples on pp. 30–31, the blank you can photocopy on p. 32. Note that I have prioritized all tasks on the sample in the left-hand column). I have also estimated (in minutes) the time I thought each task would take (the "T" for Time column) *and* noted the actual time I spent on it (in the "A" for Actual column). It's imperative you get a handle on how well you estimate homework time.

If a test is looming, make sure you can answer two key questions: How much time do I *need* to devote to studying for this exam? How much time do I *have* to study for this exam?

If you did the exercise I suggested earlier, it should be fairly easy to determine the answer to the second question. But the first question calls for a fairly definitive answer, too, or else you will never be able to plan.

Consider these other questions when figuring out the time needed:

o How much time do I usually spend studying for this type of exam? What have been the results? If you usually spend three hours and you consistently get Ds, perhaps you need to reassess the time you're spending or, more accurately, misspending.

o What grade do I have going for me now? If it's a solid B and you're convinced you can't get an A, you may decide to devote *less* time. If you have a C+ and a good grade on the exam would give you a solid B, you may decide to devote *more*.

o What special studying do I have to do? It's one thing to review notes and practice with a study group, but if you need to sit in a language lab and listen to hours of tapes or run the slower group of gerbils through the alphabet once more, plan accordingly.

o Organize the materials you need to study, pace yourself, and check to see how much material you have covered in the first hour of review. How does this compare to what you have left to study? Not every hour will be equally productive, but you should be able to project the time you need based on what you are able to accomplish in an hour.

Use the Pretest Organizer on pp. 33–34 to ensure you are completely prepared.

Be careful how you "divvy up" your valuable study time. Schedule enough time for the task, but not so much time that you burn out. Every individual is different, but most students study best in blocks of 1 hour or less, some-times as little as 20 or 30 minutes at a time, depending on the subject. You might find history fascinating and be able to read for hours. Calculus, on the other hand, may be a subject that you can best handle in small bites, a half hour at a time.

Don't overdo it. Plan your study time in blocks, break-ing up work time with short leisure activities. It's helpful to add these to your schedule as well. You'll find that these breaks help you think more clearly and creatively when you get back to studying.

Even if you tend to like longer blocks of study time, be careful about scheduling study marathons—six or eight hour stretches rather than a series of one hour sessions. The longer the period you schedule, the more likely you'll have to fight the demons of procrastination and day-dreaming. Convincing yourself that you are really studying your heart out, you'll also find it easier to justify time-wasting distractions, to schedule longer breaks, and, before long, to quit before you should.

If you find yourself fighting this demon, remind your-self (frequently) of the Law of Diminishing Returns: Your initial effort yields the biggest results, with each succeed-ing effort yielding proportionately less. And there *is* a point where even the most *prodigious* efforts yield *negli-gible* results. This applies not only to perfectionists, but also to those of you who scoff at the very thought of using a "simple" outline or producing a "formulaic" report. You do not have to always be innovative, dazzling, and cre-ative or add yet another hour of study time to the days you've already allocated to finals. Have you ever heard of an athlete who "leaves it on the practice court?" That means he is a killer during practice and a washout during games. Don't leave *your* game on the practice court by overpreparing.

When I am tempted to do far more than necessary, just because it would be a "cool" solution (and time-consuming and wasteful and inefficient and difficult), I think of George Simenon, the French author best known for his Inspector Maigret mystery series—and the *500 total books he wrote* in his lifetime. How did he do it and still have time to eat and sleep? Simple—he used only 2,000 vocabulary words (out of the 800,000 plus available to him) so he wouldn't have to interrupt his writing to consult a dictionary or thesaurus.

Listen to the chimes of your unique "study clock," then schedule the easiest tasks during nonprime hours. When your energy and motivation are at their lowest levels, should you really bore in on that project that's been giving you fits? Or merely recopy some notes, go over your calendar, or proofread a paper?

When you're least creative, least energetic and least motivated, why would you even consider tackling your most challenging assignments? Don't be like many businesspeople I know who schedule their time bass ackwards: In the morning, when they're raring to go, they read the paper, check their email, and skim trade journals. At the end of the day, when they can barely see straight, they start on the presentation for the Board of Directors' meeting...tomorrow's Board of Directors' meeting.

DON'T BE DAZED

Your long-term calendar will most likely be on the wall beside your study area (or on your desk or computer) in your dorm, apartment, or house. Your daily calendar should be carried with you so that you can add appointments and assignments as they occur. ("Oh," your teacher asks, "did I forget to tell you that we have a quiz on Friday on the first two chapters?" "Go skiing with you this weekend? With you and your gorgeous twin? Let me check my calendar!")

Carry your calendar so you minimize your chances of forgetting *anything*. Make sure you write down:

1. **Assignments due**. What has to be turned in today? Check before you leave for class. (This is like the "T" notation on my shopping list.)

2. **Errands**. Don't depend on your memory. It's not that you can't remember; it's that you don't *need* to remember. Including errands right on your calendar will help you plan ahead (e.g., actually buying a birthday present *before* your boyfriend's birthday) and save you from last-minute panic when you should be studying for an upcoming exam.

   As with any to-do list, make sure each item is really an item and not a combination of several steps (or stops). "Call Mom" is one item; "Arrange details for Spring Dance" is not.

3. **Homework**. When the teacher gives out homework assignments, here's where you can write them down so they're all together, complete with due dates, page numbers, and any other information you need to remember.

4. **Reminders**. For example, suppose your teacher tells you to meet her in a different room for your 9:30 biology class. Again, if you depend on your memory alone, you will most likely be the only one who isn't dissecting a frog over in McGillicuddy Hall. (Given the hour, that might not be a bad thing.)

In fact, you should highlight anything unusual with a bright-colored pen just to bring it to your attention. Take a moment to glance over the day's schedule twice: Look at it the night before, to psych yourself up for the coming day and ensure you didn't forget to do any special assignments. Then, glance at it again while you're having a nutritious breakfast that morning.

USING THESE TIME-SAVING TOOLS EFFECTIVELY

Organizing your life requires you to actually use these tools. Once you have discovered habits and patterns of study that work for you, continue to use and hone them.

When you're scheduling your time, be specific about which tasks you plan to do, when you plan to do them, and how long you think each will take.

Plan according to your schedule, your goals, and your aptitudes, not some ephemeral "standard." Allocate the time you expect a project to take you, not the time it might take someone else or how long your teacher says it should take. Try to be realistic and honest with yourself when determining those things that require more effort vs. those that come easier to you.

Whenever possible, schedule pleasurable activities after study time, not before. They will then act as incentives, not distractions.

Be flexible and ready to adapt. Changes happen and you'll have to adjust your schedule to accommodate them.

Monitor your progress at reasonable periods and make changes where necessary. Remember, this is your study regimen—you conceived it, you can change it.

If you find that you are consistently allotting more time than necessary to a specific chore—giving yourself an hour to review your English notes every Sunday but always finishing in 45 minutes or less—change your future schedule accordingly. You may use the extra 15 minutes for a task that consistently takes longer than you've anticipated, or just quit 15 minutes early. Isn't scheduling great?

As assignments are entered on your calendar, make sure you also enter items needed—texts, other books you have to buy, borrow, or get from the library, and special materials such as drawing pads, markers, graph paper, and so on.

You may decide that color coding your calendar—red for assignments that must be accomplished that week, blue for steps in longer-term assignments, yellow for personal time and appointments, green for classes—makes it easier for you to tell at a glance what you need to do and when you need to do it. Just don't make "coloring" a time-consuming chore.

Adapt these tools for your own use. Try anything you think may work—use it if it does, discard it if it doesn't.

Do your least favorite chores (study assignments, projects, whatever) first—you'll feel better having gotten them out of the way! Plan how to accomplish them as meticulously as possible. That will get rid of them even faster.

If you push aside the same low-priority item day after day, week after week, at some point you should just stop and decide whether it's something you need to do at all! This is a strategic way to make a task or problem "disappear."

Accomplish one task before going on to the next one—don't skip around. If you ever stuffed envelopes for a political candidate, for example, you probably learned that it is quicker and easier to sign 100 letters, then stuff them into envelopes, then seal and stamp them, than to sign, stuff, seal, and stamp one letter at a time.

If you see that you are moving along faster than you anticipated on one task or project sequence, there is absolutely nothing wrong with moving on to the next part of that assignment or the next project step.

If you are behind, don't panic. Just take the time to reorganize your schedule and find the time you need to make up. You may be able to free up time from another task or put one part of a long-term project off for a day or two. The tools we've discussed and the various other hints should get you into the habit of writing things down. Not having to remember all these items will free up space in your brain for the things you need to concentrate on or *do* have to remember.

Remember to break any long-term or difficult projects into small, "bite-size" tasks that can be included on your schedule. As Henry Ford said, "Nothing is particularly hard if you divide it into small jobs." Hence, the assembly line.

Learn to manage distractions. As a time-management axiom puts it, "Don't respond to the urgent and forget the important." Some things you do can be picked up or dropped at any time. Beware of those time-consuming and complicated tasks that, once begun, demand to be completed. Interrupting at any point might mean starting all over again. What a waste of time *that* would be!

If you're writing and you have a brainstorm just as the phone rings—and you know it's from that person you've been waiting to hear from all week—take a minute to at least jot down your ideas before you stop.

Nothing can be as counterproductive as losing your concentration, especially at critical times. Learn to ward off those enemies that would alter your course, and you will find your journey much smoother.

One way to guard against these mental intrusions is to know your own study clock and plan your study time accordingly. Each of us is predisposed to function most efficiently at specific times of day (or night). Find out what sort of study clock you're on and schedule your work during this period.

Beware of uninvited guests and all phone calls: Unless you are ready for a break, they'll only get you off schedule.

More subtle enemies include the sudden desire to sharpen every pencil in the house, an unheard-of urge to clean your room, an offer to do your sister's homework. Anything, in other words, to avoid your own work. If you find yourself ready to do anything *but* your work, either take a break then and there or pull yourself together and get down to business.

Self-discipline, too, is a learned habit that gets easier with practice. Put up your "Do not disturb" sign and stick to your guns, no matter what the temptation.

Time is relative. Car trips take longer if you have to schedule frequent stops for gas, food, and so on, longer still if you start out during rush hour. If your schedule involves working with others, take *their* sense of time into account—you may have to schedule "waiting time" for a chronically late friend...and always bring a book along.

GOING INTO "TEST TRAINING"

Now that you have discovered the value of keeping track of upcoming events, including exams—and the possibility that you can actually plan ahead and keep your life from getting too crazy even during finals week—we can talk a little about the days prior to the exams themselves.

If you have an upcoming exam early in the morning and you are afraid you won't be in shape for it, do a bit of subterfuge on your body and brain.

Get up early for several days before the exam, have a good breakfast, and do homework or review your notes. This will help jump start your brain and get it used to the idea of solving equations or thinking seriously about Shakespeare at an earlier-than-usual hour.

At the end of the day, take care to get to bed early enough. Forego the late-night parties and the midnight movies on TV and actually get some serious zzzzzs.

CRAMMING DOESN'T WORK

In case I didn't mention it yet, *cramming does not work.* We've all done it at one time or another, with one excuse or another—waited until the last minute and then tried to fit a week's, month's, or entire semester's worth of work into a single night or weekend. Did it work? Doubt it.

After a night of no sleep and too much coffee, most of us are lucky if we remember where the test *is* the next day. A few hours later, trying to stay awake long enough to make it back to bed, we not only haven't learned anything, we haven't done well on the test we crammed for!

HOW TO CRAM ANYWAY

Nevertheless, despite your resolve, best intentions, and firm conviction that cramming is a losing proposition, you may well find yourself—though hopefully not too often—in the position of needing to do *some*thing the night before a test you haven't studied for at all. If so, there are some rules to follow that will make your night of cramming at least marginally successful.

Be realistic about what you can do. You absolutely *cannot* master a semester's worth of work in one night. The *more* you try to cram in, the *less* effective you will be.

Be selective and study in depth. The more you've missed, the more selective you must be in organizing your cram session. You *can't* study it all. In this case, it's better to know a lot about a little rather than a little about a lot.

Massage your memory. Use every memory technique you know (and those in **Improve Your Memory**) to maximize what you can retain.

Know when to give up. When you can't remember your name or see the page in front of you, give up and get some sleep.

Consider an early-morning versus a late-night cram. Especially if you're a morning person, but even if you're not, I've found it more effective to go to bed and get up early rather than go to bed late and get up exhausted.

Spend the first few minutes of the test writing down whatever you remember now but are afraid you'll forget.

Get a copy of another of my books—Last Minute Study Tips. It will help you prepare for a test that's weeks, days, hours, or just minutes away...and do better on it.

As TIME GOES BY

Be honest with yourself. Don't block out two hours to study for your calculus exam *today* when you suspect your best friend will entice you to go with him to get a pizza and talk about anything *but* calculus. If you have budgeted six hours to prepare for the entire exam, you've just cheated yourself out of a third of the time.

It's okay to write down "pizza with Binky" for those two hours. Just be realistic and honest and budget your study time when you will truly be studying.

STUDYING WITH KIDS

Since many of you are going to school while raising a family, I want to add some particular tidbits of advice for studying when screaming munchkins are gnawing at your legs.

Plan activities to keep the kids occupied. The busier you are in school or at work, the more time your kids will want from you when you *are* home. If you spend a little time with them, it may be easier for them to play alone, especially if you've created projects *they* can work on while *you're* working on your homework.

Make the kids part of your study routine. Kids love routine, so include them in yours. If 5:30 to 7:30 is "Dad's Study Time," they'll get used to it, especially if you make spending other time with them a priority and give them something to do during those hours. Explain what you're doing in a way that includes an ultimate benefit for them—it'll motivate *them* to be part of your "study team."

Use the television as a babysitter. While many of you disapprove of this, it may be the lesser of two evils.

Plan your study accordingly. Take more frequent breaks to spend five minutes with your kids. They'll be more likely to give you the 15 or 20 minutes at a time you need if they get periodic attention themselves. By default, that means delaying projects that require an hour or more of massive concentration until the darlings have been put to bed.

Find help. Spouses can occasionally take the kids out for dinner and a movie, relatives can babysit at their homes on a rotating basis, playmates can be invited over (allowing you to send yours to *their* house another day), you may be able to trade babysitting chores with other parents at school, and professional day care may be available at your child's school or in someone's home.

Sample (Filled-in) Long-term Calendar

MONTH: *January*

MON	TUE	WED	THU	FRI	SAT	SUN
1	2 *Gorbachev rough paper due*	3	4	5 *French vocab quiz*	6 *Mom visit →*	7 ~
8	9 *English midterm*	10 *Geometry midterm*	11 *History midterm*	12	13	14
15	16	17	18	19	20 *Lacrosse tourney ~*	21
22	23	24 *First 2 parts of French project due*	25	26 *French vocab quiz*	27 *Lacrosse tourney ~*	28 ~
29	30	31				

Blank Long-term Calendar

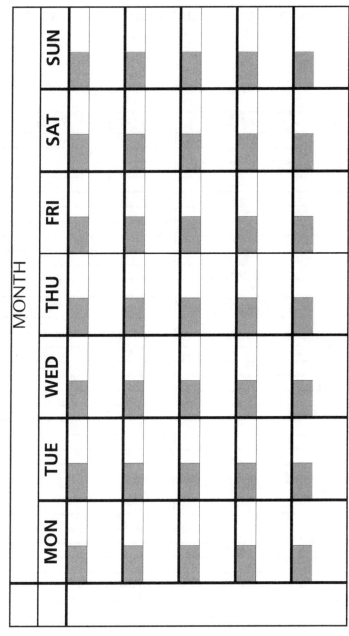

Sample (Filled-in) Daily Calendar

January

20	Monday		T	A	Notes
A	Geometry	probs 24-42 odd	40	60	pick up milk & eggs
A	History	Read CH. 3	30	40	Don't forget homework!
A	Biology	Finish lab report	60	25	
		Read CH 8	30	25	
C	Choose English topic		20	15	
	Check with teacher		10	10	
A	Bring gym shorts tomorrow				
B	Call Cheryl right after sch.				
A	7PM Band rehearsal		120	180	

21	Tuesday		T	A	Notes
C	Health Redo chart (due Fri)		30	20	
A	Geometry	24-42 Even	40	70	
B	Spanish	Essay rough draft	75	120	See Mr. Dawkins for
					Thursday Appt.
B	Band 6:30		120	150	

22	Wednesday		T	A	Notes
A	Spanish	Essay final draft	60	70	
		proof	30	30	
A	History	Chap 4	30	45	
B	Biology	Chap 9	30	45	
		probs p.112	50	30	

Sample (Filled-in) Daily Calendar (Cont'd)

January

23	Thursday	T	A	Notes
A	Finalize Health chart, proof	20	40	
B	research English paper	120	0	2:30 Mr. Dawkins
	(online)			@ Lib. office
				Bring gym shorts!
				Dr. Gevens 5PM
	Band 6:30	60	150	

24	Friday	T	A	Notes
B	Geometry probs 85-110	50	90	
				Jerry - Are u picking me
				up tonight?
				What time?
				Bring PJs
	Call: Rob 742-6891			Toothbrush
	Jack 742-2222			Makeup
	Ira 743-8181			CDs (see list)
	Cheryl 777-7777			

25	Saturday	T	A	Notes
A	Study for Geometry quiz	120	90	
B	Study for Hist. midterm	120	120	
	(Feb 3)			
A	Biology probs pp. 113-114	60	45	

26	Sunday	T	A	Notes
	ENJOY!			
				Call mom!
	Church 11AM			
	Brunch @ Amy's 2PM			

Blank Daily Calendar

		T	A	Notes

		T	A	Notes

		T	A	Notes

Pretest Organizer

Class: _____ **Teacher:** _____

    Test date: ____ **Time:** From:_____ To: _____

    Place: _____

Special instructions to myself (e.g., take calculator, dictionary, etc.):

_____

_____

_____

Materials I need to study for this test (check all needed):

_____ Book   _____ Tapes/videos

_____ Workbook   _____ Old tests

_____ Class notes   _____ Other

_____ Handouts

Format of the test (write the number of T/F, essays, and so forth, and total points for each section):

_____

_____

_____

_____

_____

_____

Study group meetings (times, places):

1. _____

2. _____

3. _____

4. _____

5. _____

Material to be covered:

Indicate topics, sources, and amount of review (light or heavy) required. Check box when review is completed.

Topic	Sources	Review
____	____	____
____	____	____
____	____	____
____	____	____
____	____	____
____	____	____
____	____	____

After the test:

Grade I expected _____ Grade I received _____
What did I do that helped me?

_____

_____

_____

_____

_____

What else should I have done?

_____

_____

_____

_____

_____

_____

_____

_____

When Should You Start Studying?

"HE LISTENS WELL WHO TAKES NOTES."
—*DANTE*

● ● ●

Once upon a time, there was a hard-working student named Kyle. He read his textbooks, took good notes in class, rarely missed a day of school, and always did his homework. Sitting next to him in class was a guy named Brent. This guy *sort of* took notes, *kind of* read his textbook, and *usually* did his homework. Well, okay, not usually, but *kind of* usually—if he came to class at all.

The day of the big test came. Hard-working Kyle got a D and slouchy, lazy Brent got an A.

If you believe this bears any resemblance to reality, please read and reread every one of the books in my **How to Study Program**. You need all the help you can get.

This story reveals what I really want to emphasize in this chapter: You don't start preparing for a test a couple of days before. You begin when you walk into the classroom on the first day—or even *before* that.

Everything you do in that course—attending class, applying listening skills, taking good notes, doing your homework, and reading all the assignments—is part and parcel of your "studying" for the exam.

FOR WHOM THE ALARM CLOCK TOLLS

Yes, my friend, it may be cruel and it may be cold, but getting out of bed and going to class is the first step toward passing the final that's four months away.

"Missing that biology class just this one time can't huuuuurrrrrt!" you moan as you roll over and bury your head under the pillow.

Obviously, if this is you, you've got to start by getting to bed a little bit earlier, planning ahead a little bit more, and deciding that going to class is something you must do automatically.

Oh, and if you're in college, be smart and *don't* schedule early morning classes if you can barely see straight before noon!

NOW THAT YOU'RE HERE...

All right. I got you out of bed and inside the classroom. You're awake, polite, respectful, and listening. Now what?

Actually, that question should have been asked last night or several nights ago. When you arrive, your teacher expects you to have:

1. Read the assignment.
2. Brought your notes/textbooks.

3. Brought your homework assignment.

4. Opened your notebook to the right page, opened the textbook to the current chapter, and taken out your homework to hand it in.

Before that bell rings for class to begin, have your work ready to go so you don't waste time trying to find everything. Of course, if you've done a last-minute check back home or in the dorm, you'll know for sure that you've got the right books, notebooks, homework assignments, and so forth. Teachers get really tired of hearing, "I left it at home/in the car/in the dorm/with my girlfriend."

My daughter Lindsay was notorious for forgetting homework assignments...or forgetting to bring in those she had actually done. I solved the problem by handing her a bright red manila folder marked "HOMEWORK," into which she shoved every assignment the instant it was done. And I overhauled her calendar so she stopped "forgetting" so many assignments in the first place.

POP GOES THE QUIZ

Not all tests, as you know by now, are announced. Your teacher may decide, out of malice, boredom, or his lesson plan book, to give you a pop quiz.

How can you score well if, first of all, you aren't in class and, second of all, haven't read the new material and periodically reviewed the old? And suppose it's an open-book test...and you don't have a book to open?

Let's face it. Biology, U.S. history, economics, or whatever 101 may not be your favorite subject, but that doesn't mean you have to have an attitude about it. "Proving" you can't or won't do well in a class proves nothing.

THE NEXT STEPS

Let's move on to what you should do during class, after class and before class.

Taking effective notes during class requires five separate actions on your part:

1. *Listening* actively.
2. *Selecting* pertinent information.
3. *Condensing* it.
4. *Sorting/organizing* it.
5. *Interpreting* it (later).

So, during class, you need to listen and observe. Not a difficult task, even when the teacher isn't going to win any elocution or acting awards. Identifying noteworthy material means finding a way to separate the wheat—that which you *should* write down—from the chaff—that which you should *ignore*.

How do you do that? By *listening* for verbal clues and *watching* for nonverbal ones.

Many teachers will invariably signal important material in the way they present it—pausing (waiting for all the pens to rise), repeating the same point, slowing down their normally supersonic lecture speed, speaking more loudly (or more softly), or even by simply stating, "I think the following is important."

There are also a number of words that should *signal* noteworthy material (and, at the same time, give you the clues you need to organize your notes logically): "first of all," "most importantly," "therefore," "as a result," "to summarize," "on the other hand," "on the contrary," "the following (number of) reasons (causes, effects, decisions, facts, and so forth)."

Other words and phrases alert you to write down the lecture material that follows and help you put it in context—to make a list ("first," "the following reasons"); establish a cause-and-effect relationship ("therefore," "as a result"); establish opposites or alternatives ("on the other hand," "on the contrary," "alternatively"); signify a conclusion ("therefore," "to summarize"); or offer an explanation or definition.

Don't Just Listen, Watch!

If the teacher begins looking out the window or his eyes glaze over, he's sending you a clear signal: "This isn't going to be on the test (so don't take notes!)."

On the other hand, if she turns to write something on the blackboard, makes eye contact with several students, and/or gestures dramatically, she's sending an even clearer signal about the importance of the point she's making.

Of course, there are many exceptions to this rule. My first-year calculus instructor would occasionally launch into long diatribes about his mother or air pollution, with tones more impassioned than any he used for differential equations.

There was also the trigonometry professor I endured who got all worked up about the damage being done to the nation's sidewalks by the deadly menace of chewing gum.

Nevertheless, learn to be a detective—don't overlook the clues.

Teachers like to see students take notes. It shows them that you're interested in the topic at hand and think enough of what is being said to write it down. (If you've ever stood at the front of the room, you can usually tell who's taking notes and who's writing a letter to a friend in Iowa.)

You are your own best note taker

I'm sure you've observed in your classes that some people are constantly taking notes. Others end up with two lines on one page. Most of us fall in between.

The person who never stops taking notes is either writing a letter to that friend in Iowa or has absolutely no idea what *is* or is *not* important.

The result is dozens of pages of notes (by the end of the semester) that may or may not be helpful. This person is so busy writing down stuff that he isn't prepared or even aware that he can ask and answer questions to help him understand the material better. To use that old adage, he can't see the forest for the trees. He is probably the same person who takes a marking pen and underlines or highlights every word in his textbook.

Compare him to the guy who thinks note taking isn't cool, so he only writes down today's date and the homework assignment. He may write something when the teacher says, "Now, write this down and remember it," but probably just scribbles some nonsense words. After all, he's cool.

Watch him sweat when it's time to study for the exam. He's stuck with a faulty memory and a textbook that may not contain half the material that will be on the test.

Take notes on what you don't know

You *know* the first lines of Hamlet's soliloquy. You *know* the Pythagorean Theorem. You *know* what date Columbus "discovered" America. So why waste time and space writing them down?

Frequently, your teachers will present material you already know in order to set the stage for further discussion or introduce material that is more difficult. Don't be so conditioned to automatically copy down dates, vocabulary, terms, formulas, and names that you mindlessly take notes on information you already know. You'll just be wasting your time—both in class and later, when you review your overly detailed notes.

Items discussed during any lesson can be grouped into several categories, which vary in importance:

- Information not contained in the class texts and other assigned readings.
- Explanations of obscure material covered in the texts and readings but with which students might be having difficulty.
- Demonstrations or examples that provide greater understanding of the subject matter.
- Background information that puts the course material in context.

As you are listening to an instructor, decide in which category the information being presented belongs. This will help you determine how detailed your notes should be. (It will become easier to do this as you get to know the instructor.)

LOOKS AREN'T EVERYTHING, BUT...

You don't have to be a master of shorthand to streamline your note taking. Here are five ways:

1. Eliminate vowels. As a sign that was ubiquitous in the New York City subways used to proclaim, "If u cn rd ths, u cn gt a gd jb." (If you can read this, you can get a good job.)

2. Use word beginnings ("rep" for representative, "con" for Congressperson), and other easy-to-remember abbreviations.

3. Stop putting periods after all abbreviations (they add up!).

4. Use standard symbols in place of words. Here is a list that will help you out in most of your classes. (You may recognize many of these symbols from your math and logic courses.)

≈	approximately
w/	with
w/o	without
wh/	which
→	resulting in
←	as a result of/consequence of
+	and or also
*	most importantly
cf	compare; in comparison; in relation to
ff	following
<	less than
>	more than
=	the same as
↑	increasing
↓	decreasing
esp	especially
Δ	change
⊂	it follows that
∴	therefore
b/c	because

5. Create your own symbols and abbreviations based on your needs and comfort level.

There are three symbols I think you'll want to create—they'll be needed again and again:

W That's my symbol for "What?" as in "What the heck does that mean?"; "What did she say?"; or "What happened? I'm completely lost!" It denotes something that's been missed—leave space in your notes to fill in the missing piece of the puzzle after class.

M That's my symbol for "My thought." I want to separate my thoughts during a lecture from the professor's—mix in too many of your own ideas (without noting they are yours) and you will invariably get mixed up.

T! My symbol for "Test!" as in "He actually said this is going to be on the test. How about you study it, dummy!!!"

While I recommend using all these basic symbols and abbreviations *all* the time, in *every* class, in order to maintain consistency you may want to create specific symbols or abbreviations for each class. In chemistry, "TD" may stand for thermodynamics, and "K" for the Kinetic Theory of Gases (but don't confuse it with the K for Kelvin). In history, "GW" is the father of our country, "ABE" is Mr. Honesty, "FR" could be French Revolution (or "freedom rider"), and "IR" is Industrial Revolution.

To TAPE OR NOT TO TAPE

I am opposed to using a tape recorder in class as a substitute for an active brain for the following reasons:

○ **It's time consuming**, since you'll have to listen to the same lecture at least twice.

○ **It's virtually useless for review**. Fast forwarding and rewinding cassettes to find the salient points of a lecture is torture. During the hectic days before an exam, do you really want to waste time listening to a whole lecture when you could just reread your notes?

○ **It offers no backup**. Only the most diligent students will record *and* take notes. But what happens if your tape recorder malfunctions? How useful will blank or distorted tapes be to you when it's time to review? If you're going to take notes as a backup, why not just take good notes and leave the tape recorder home?

○ **It costs money**. Compare the price of blank paper and a pen to that of recorder, batteries, and tapes. The cost of batteries *alone* should convince you that you're better off going the low-tech route.

○ **You miss the "live" clues we discussed earlier**. When all you have is a tape of your lecture, you don't see that zealous flash in your teacher's eyes, the passionate arm flailing, the stern set of the jaw, any and all of which should scream, "Pay attention. I guarantee this will be on your test!"

READING IS FUNDAMENTAL

Reading improves reading. If you hate reading or consider yourself a slow reader, keep at it anyway. Read anything and everything. Read at night and on weekends. Read cereal boxes and newspapers and magazines and short stories and...well, you get the idea.

As you may have guessed by now, there's a volume in my **How to Study Program** on this topic, too. It's called **Improve Your Reading** (available in a brand new fifth edition), and it gives you a simple action plan to read faster and remember more.

Let's look at how you can use your reading skills—and improve them—to get higher grades. Here are some suggestions that will help you read more efficiently:

When a chapter in a textbook has questions at the end, read the questions first. Why? They will give you an idea of what the chapter is all about, "clues" that scream out what to look for in the text.

Some of the words in each chapter will help you identify the important points and ignore the unimportant. Knowing when to speed up, slow down, ignore, or really concentrate will help you read both faster and more effectively.

When you see words such as "likewise," "in addition," "moreover," "furthermore," and the like, you should know nothing new is being introduced. If you already know what's going on, speed up or skip what's coming entirely.

When you see words such as "on the other hand," "nevertheless," "however," "rather," "but," and their ilk, slow down—you're getting information that adds a new perspective or contradicts what you've just read.

Lastly, watch out for payoff words such as, "in conclusion," "to summarize," "consequently," "thus"—especially if you only have time to hit the high points of a chapter.

Underline or highlight main points in the text. At the same time, pay special attention to words and phrases the author has highlighted by placing them in italics or in boldface.

Don't skip over the maps, charts, graphs, photos, or drawings. Much of this information may not be repeated in the text. If you skip it, you may be missing vital information.

What's the big picture here? We can get bogged down in the footnotes and unfamiliar words and lose touch with the purpose of the chapter. Keep these simple steps in mind:

If there is a heading, rephrase it as a question. This will support your purpose for reading.

Examine all subheadings, illustrations, and graphics, as these will help you identify the significant matter within the text.

Read the introductory paragraphs, summary, and any questions at the end of the chapter.

Read the first sentence of every paragraph. This is generally where the main idea is found.

Evaluate what you've gained from the process: Can you answer the questions at the chapter's end? Could you intelligently participate in a class discussion of the material?

Write a brief summary of what you have learned from your skimming.

Shortly before class, look over the chapter again. Review what you and the author have decided are the most important points and mark topics you want the teacher to explain.

15 QUESTIONS TO HELP YOU

Beyond grasping the meaning of words and phrases, critical reading requires that you ask questions. Here are 15 questions that will help you effectively analyze and interpret most of what you read:

1.   Is a clear message communicated throughout?
2.   Are the relationships between the points direct and clear?
3.   Is there a relationship between your experience and the author's?
4.   Are the details factual?
5.   Are the examples and evidence relevant?
6.   Is there consistency of thought?
7.   What is the author's bias or slant?
8.   What is the author's motive?
9.   What does the author want you to believe?
10.   Does this jibe with your beliefs or experiences?
11.   Is the author rational or subjective?
12.   Is there a confusion between feelings and facts?
13.   Are the main points logically ordered?
14.   Are the arguments and conclusions consistent?
15.   Are the explanations clear?

Obviously, this list of questions is not all-inclusive, but it will give you a jump start when critical reading is required. Remember, the essential ingredient to any effective analysis and interpretation is the questions you ask.

AFTER CLASS

The best time to study for your next class is right after the last one. Say you have American history at 9:30 a.m. on Tuesday and Thursday. As soon as you can after your Tuesday class, review the day's notes, type them if possible, and complete the reading and homework for Thursday.

Why? Because the class is fresh in your mind. Your notes are crying out to be reviewed and corrected or added to, and you have a level of understanding that may not be there Wednesday night at 9 p.m.

Then, spend a little time on the same class and the same materials just before the next class. Let's say you can do that at 8:30 a.m. on Thursday. The *big* study time is ASAP after Tuesday's class; the little *quick-let's-review* time comes shortly *before* Thursday's class.

Now, let's refine these study habits for the next test.

Study Smarter, Not Harder

"YOU HAVE TO STUDY A GREAT DEAL TO KNOW A LITTLE."
—CHARLES DE SECONDAT, BARON DE MONTESQUIEU

I'm going to be so bold as to amend what the baron said: "You have to study a reasonable amount to know a great deal." Why change his centuries-old words? Because we know a lot about study techniques that he didn't. We should (and can) find ways to study smarter, not harder.

ESTABLISH YOUR STUDY ROUTINE

As much as possible, create a routine time of day to study. Some students find it easier to set aside specific blocks of time for study during the day—every day. In reality, the time of day *you* should do your work will be determined by a number of factors:

1. **Study when you're at your best.** What is your "peak performance period"—the time of day you do your best work? This varies from person to person—

you may be dead to the world 'til noon but able to study well into the night. Or maybe you're up and alert at the crack of dawn but distracted and tired if you try to burn the midnight oil.

2. **Consider your sleep habits**. Habit is a powerful influence. If you always set your alarm for 7 a.m., you may find that you wake up then even if you forget to set it. If you are used to going to sleep around 11 p.m., you will undoubtedly get quite tired if you try to stay up studying until 2 a.m., and probably accomplish very little during those three extra hours.

3. **Study when you can**. Although you want to study when you're mentally most alert, external factors also play a role in deciding when you study. Being at your best is not always possible: Study whenever circumstances allow.

4. **Consider the complexity of the assignment when you allocate time**. The tasks themselves may have a great effect on your schedule. You will need to spend more time on subjects in which you're having trouble, while you may breeze through assignments others have trouble with.

WHERE SHOULD YOU STUDY?

If you've never asked yourself this question—assuming that home is where the heart and the books are—take the time to discover both where you're most comfortable and most effective. Here are some possibilities:

At the library. There may be numerous choices, from the large reading room, to quieter, sometimes deserted specialty rooms, to your own study cubicle.

At home. Just remember that this is the place where distractions are most likely to occur. No one tends to telephone you at the library and little brothers (or your own kids) will not tend to find you easily in the "stacks."

At a friend's, neighbor's, or relative's house. This may not be an option for most of you, even on an occasional basis, but you may want to set up one or two alternative study sites.

In an empty classroom. Certainly an option at many colleges and perhaps some private high schools, it is a good idea mainly because so few students have ever thought of it!

At your job. Whether you're a student working part-time or fully employed and going to school part-time, you may be able to make arrangements to use an empty office, even during regular office hours, or perhaps after everyone has left (depending on how much your boss trusts you). If you're in junior high or high school and a parent, friend, or relative works nearby, you may be able to work from the end of school until closing time at their workplace.

Stay Focused on Your Studies

Whatever location you choose as your "study base," how you set up your study area can affect your ability to stay focused and, if you aren't careful, seriously inhibit quality study time.

If you find yourself doodling and dawdling more than diagramming and deciphering, consider these solutions:

Create a work environment in which you're comfortable. The size, style, and placement of your desk, chair, and lighting may all affect whether you're distracted from the work at hand. Take the time to design the area that's perfect for you. Needless to say, anything that you know will distract you—a girlfriend's picture, a radio or TV, whatever, should disappear from your study area.

Turn up the lights. Experiment with the placement and intensity of lighting until you find what works for you, both in terms of comfort and as a means of staying awake and focused.

Set some rules. Let family, relatives, and especially friends know how important your studying is and that specific hours are inviolate.

Take the breaks you need. Don't follow some parent's or teacher's well-intentioned but bogus advice about how long you should study before taking a break. Take breaks when *you* need to.

WAKE UP!!!

You've chosen the best study spot and no one could fault you on its setup. So why are you still using pencils to prop open your eyelids? Help is on the way.

Take a nap. What a concept! When you're too tired to study, take a short nap to revive yourself. The key is to maximize that nap's effect, and *that* means keeping it short—20 to 40 minutes.

Have a drink. A little caffeine won't harm you—a cup of coffee or tea, a glass of soda. A case of Red Bull might be overkill.

Turn down the heat. You needn't build an igloo, but too warm a room will leave you dreaming of sugarplums.

Shake a leg. Or anything else that peps you up. Go for a walk, high step around the kitchen, do jumping jacks—even mild physical exertion will give you an immediate lift.

Change your study schedule. Presuming you have some choice here, find a way to study when you are normally more awake and/or more efficient.

The Pharaohs Would Approve

Now I'll tell you about my Inverted Pyramid Theory.

The top is very wide, the bottom very narrow. This is symbolic of the way you should study for a test. Begin with all possible materials (all notes, book chapters, workbooks, audiotapes, and so forth) and briefly review everything to see what you need to spend time with and what you can put aside.

I also call this separating the wheat from the chaff. The wheat is the edible good stuff that's taken from the field and turned into Chocolate Sugar Munchies. The chaff stays behind. Now try this:

1. Gather all the material you have been using for the course: books, workbooks, handouts, notes, homework, and previous tests and papers.

2. Compare the contents with the material you will be tested on and ask yourself: What exactly do I need to review for this test?

3. Select the material for review. Reducing the pile of books and papers will be a psychological aid—

suddenly, it'll seem as if you have enough time and energy to study for the test.

4. Photocopy and complete the Pretest Organizer on pp. 33–34. Consider carefully the "Material to be covered" section. Be specific. The more detailed you are, the better job you'll do reviewing all the areas that you should know. This exercise will help you *quantify* what you need to do.

5. As you review the material and conclude that you know it for the test, put a bold check mark on the "Okay" line. You are, to use my example, inverting the pyramid—shrinking the amount of material you need to study.

    Now you have time not only to spend on the stuff that's giving you grief, but to seek out other sources (fellow students, the teacher, the library) and get to the heart of the matter.

6. By the time the test is given, you should have reduced the "pyramid" to nothing. Go into the test and do well!

7. Hot tip: Make a crib sheet as if you were going to cheat on the test, which, of course, you are not. Use it for last-minute review. And if you are lucky enough to get an open-book test, thank me!

YOU WANT TO READ IT AGAIN?

You neither have time nor a valid reason to reread *all* the material in your textbook or lecture notes. You *do* need to skim and scan it to pull out the essence and remind yourself of the main points.

Skimming is reading fast for an overview, for general information. Scanning is reading fast to find specifics. Both emphasize "fast" and "reading." You don't flip the pages of the book so quickly that you get a chill from the breeze, but you don't start reading the book again either.

Look at what you've underlined and highlighted. Look at boldfaced and italicized words, subheads, captions, questions—all in all, the "meat" of the chapter.

You're going to use the same reading methods with the other study material, including your notes. Your notes, however, should probably receive the most careful attention, since they will reflect the teacher's lectures and her viewpoints and biases, as well as key buzzwords.

The Way of All Flash

You probably remember flash cards from elementary school. On one side was a picture, on the other a word. Or one side held a definition ("Someone who studies bugs"), and the other the word being defined ("entomologist").

Using flash cards is a great way to test yourself. It also works for two people studying together or for a group. Flash cards are effective for studying vocabulary, short answers, definitions, matching ("Boise" and "potato"), and facts in preparation for a true/false tests.

No Person Is an Island

Share *your* knowledge while you benefit from the knowledge of a handful of other students in the same class. In other words, form a study group.

Try to study with others who are at your level or slightly above. Notice I say *slightly* above. If you're a solid C and they're easy-A people, you won't connect. You'll want to review information they'll agree to skip. (The opposite will happen to *you* if you choose people too far below you.)

Study groups can be organized in a variety of ways. Each member could be assigned primary responsibility for a single class, including preparing detailed notes from lectures and discussion groups. If supplementary reading is recommended but not required, that person could be responsible for doing all such reading and preparing detailed summaries.

The extra work you will have to do in one class will be offset by the extra work others will be doing for you.

Alternatively, everybody can be responsible for his or her own notes, but the group could act as an ad hoc discussion group, refining your understanding of key points, working on problems, questioning each other, practicing for tests, and so forth.

Even if you find only one or two other students willing to work with you, such cooperation will be invaluable, especially in preparing for major exams.

I suggest four students minimum, probably six maximum. You want to ensure each person gets a chance to participate as much as he or she wants while maximizing the collective knowledge and wisdom of the group.

While group members needn't be best friends, they shouldn't be overtly hostile to one another, either. Seek diversity of experience, demand common dedication. Avoid a group in which you're the "star"—at least until you flicker out during the first exam.

Decide early on if you're forming a study group or a social group. If it's the latter, don't pretend it's the former. If it's the former, don't just invite your friends and informally sit around discussing what happened on "The OC" last week.

Make meeting times and assignments formal and rigorous. Consider rigid rules of conduct. Ditch nonserious students early. You don't want anyone who is working as little as possible and taking advantage of *your* hard work.

However you choose to organize, clearly decide—early on—the exact requirements and assignments of each student. Again, you never want the feeling to emerge that one or two of you are trying to "ride the coattails" of the others.

LEARN FROM YOUR MISTAKES

If you have access to old exams written by the same teacher, especially if they cover the same material you're going to be tested on, use *them* for review.

Don't expect the same questions to appear again. No teacher is *that* accommodating. But the way the test is prepared, the kinds of questions employed, and the mix of questions (100 true/false, 50 multiple choice and one—count 'em—one essay) will give a much better idea of what to expect on your test.

At the same time, see if you can find anyone who had this teacher last year or last semester. Can they give you any advice, tips, hints, or warnings?

Once you've discovered the type of test facing you, you need to figure out what's going to be *on* it (and hence, what you need to study). Remember, it's rarely, if ever, "everything."

At most, do a cursory review of material you are convinced is simply not important enough to be included on an upcoming test. This will automatically give you more time to concentrate on those areas you're sure *will* be included.

Then create a "To Study" sheet for each test. On it, list specific books to review, notes to recheck, and topics, principles, ideas, and concepts to go over. This method will minimize procrastination, logically organize your studying, and give you ongoing "jolts" of accomplishment as you complete each item.

ALL TEACHERS ARE NOT EQUAL (OR FAIR OR NICE OR...)

In an ideal world, all teachers would be filled with knowledge they eagerly and expertly shared with their students. Their lectures would be exciting and brief. Their tests would be fair and accurate measurements of what the students should have learned.

There *are* a lot of teachers out there like that. If you don't think you've had one yet, your turn is coming.

In the meantime, though, let's consider the kind of teacher you're probably more familiar with, who seems to take particular glee in preparing tests that are difficult, sometimes even downright unfair. If you're lucky, you'll be forewarned by former students. If not, the first test will certainly wake you up.

Watch for these danger signs. Even if he never seems to know when the next test will be, try to get that answer out of him. Believe me, you want to ask. It's better to discover today that it's a week from Thursday than find out the Wednesday before.

If he says he doesn't know what the test will cover, keep asking him. Also ask what types of questions will be on the test (true/false, multiple choice, essays) and what percentage of the test will be devoted to each. By your questions, you are helping him shape the test in his mind, and giving him the information he needs to give back to you.

Once you've taken the test, check your corrected paper carefully. If a right answer was marked wrong, let him know. If a question was ambiguous and you think your answer *could* be right as well as the one *he* says is right, let him know. If you can explain your reasoning logically, most teachers will consider giving you at least partial credit.

It's Just the SAT. Relax.

Well, you did it. You registered to take the SAT, the ACT, or some other supposedly life-altering test, and the Day of Reckoning is approaching.

While I'll share some specifics on taking *any* test in the next few chapters, for right now just remember that any hours-long national standardized test requires a lot of the same skills and the same planning as any unit quiz, chapter test, midterm, or final.

Since these standardized tests are intended to test your general knowledge of many areas, rather than grill you on the details from Chapter 14 of your chemistry book, you cannot study specific material.

This test will seek to find out what you know about a lot of different subjects. Some of the answers will come from knowledge you gained years before. Others will come from your ability to work out the problems right there, using techniques and knowledge you gained this semester.

To prepare for any standardized test—the SAT, ACT, GRE, GMAT, and so forth—I have one big suggestion: Determine, based on your past test-taking experiences and your comfort levels, what your weak areas are. Do you continually and completely mess up essay questions? Do analogies spin you out of control? Do you freeze at the sight of an isosceles triangle?

Seek out teachers, librarians, and school counselors who can guide you to samples of these kinds of questions. Ask your teachers and fellow students for advice on handling the areas in which you're weak, take the sample tests, then work on evaluating how you did. Keep testing yourself, and keep evaluating how you are doing.

Get advice from other students who say things like, "Analogies? Piece of cake!" Find out if they really can do them easily and get tips from them (and from what I say in the following chapters).

Also, a solid review of basic math and English will be valuable. If geometry is not your strong suit, find a book that contains lists of the fundamentals and spend time reviewing information that you will be expected to exercise on the SAT. Do the same with the other subject areas to be tested.

You've probably been told for most of your life that your score on the SAT will determine whether you become a raving success eating in the finest restaurants or the busboy who cleans up afterwards. How vital is the SAT to the college admission process and, one presumes, to the rest of your life? Depending on whom you listen to, "very" or "not at all."

According to Michele Hernandez, a former admissions officer at Dartmouth (quoted in the January 10, 1999, *New York Times Magazine*), "Deep down, admissions officers don't want SAT scores to count that much, but...they do." Yet more than 300 colleges no longer even require the SAT or ACT for admission, believing it's more important that they assess a student's real level of learning and effort, not their "innate ability."

Be aware that major changes in the SAT—the first since 1994—are being introduced in March, 2005. It will now consist of *three* sections: Writing (multiple-choice questions about grammar and usage and an essay); Critical Reading (formerly the "Verbal" section); and Math.

The new Writing section will take 1 hour—35 minutes for multiple choice questions and 25 minutes to write an essay which will require you to take a position on an issue and use examples to support it. This section will be marked (as the Verbal and Math sections still will be) on a scale from 200 to 800, so a perfect SAT score is now 2,400. The SAT II: Writing Test is being eliminated as of January, 2005.

The Critical Reading section will take 70 minutes, broken down into two 25-minute sections and one 20-minute section. Analogies have been eliminated. Sentence completion questions and long reading passages remain. Short reading passages are being added.

The Math section will also consist of two 25-minute sections and one 20-minute section. Quantitative comparison questions have been eliminated, but more advanced topics from algebra II—such as exponential growth, absolute value, and functional notation—are being added. Calculators are still permitted (though it is still possible to solve every question without one).

As a result of these changes, the test will now take 3 hours and 45 minutes, 30 minutes longer than previous SAT exams.

Just to make sure everyone is confused, while some changes will be made to the PSAT, typically taken as practice by sophomores and juniors, it will include neither an essay nor advanced math. Go figure.

To BE OR NOT TO BE (COACHED)?

Should you take one of those SAT preparation courses? Is it worth the money, the time, the effort, the bother? According to a past study by the Educational Testing Service, which administers the SAT for the College Board, coached students who took the test twice or more increased their verbal score by 29 points, math by 40. Uncoached students showed an increase of 21 points on the verbal and 22 on math. These are the figures the College Board cites to claim that coaching does not really help.

Which is why, I guess, they offer an SAT PrepPack for online practice and review and a software package called One-on-One with the SAT.

So the answer is a definite maybe. Ask others for recommendations. Listen closely to why they liked or disliked a particular course. Ask about each course's effectiveness and specific results.

Evaluate the professionalism of whatever course you're considering. How good are the materials? Do they look complete and professionally prepared, or do they consist of a sheaf of badly photocopied forms and a ratty binder? Can you attend a free meeting to get a feel for the procedures? Will they furnish you with the resumes of your instructors? Will those instructors be accessible outside of class?

Finally, are there any money-back guarantees? The best companies—in this or any field—stand behind their product, even if that means giving full refunds to dissatisfied customers.

The standardized test coaching programs should deal with two areas—method and content.

Method is the study of *how* to take a test, specifically how to take the SAT, ACT, GRE, or whichever standardized test you happen to be preparing for. That portion of the course will cover much of the same material that you're reading in this book, especially what we're going to cover in the next two chapters.

Content deals with practicing the sort of stuff that will be on the specific test you are taking—vocabulary words, math problems, essay questions, and so on.

Practicing for the SAT by answering questions that are similar in content to the "real deal" is a valuable exercise, but it's only half the equation. The other half is the feedback you get from your coach (or teacher, counselor, or fellow students) on what you did, how you did it, and why you did what you did.

Many standardized tests are no longer offered "on paper," only on computer (CAT—for computer-adaptive testing format). Among the most important in this category are the GMAT (Graduate Management Admissions Test), GRE (Graduate Record Exam), and TOEFL (Test of English as a Foreign Language), along with a number of specific licensing tests.

What does this mean to you? Tests available only in CAT format require a different strategy because of two important factors: You can't return to a previous answer and you can't skip a question and return to it later. Make sure you know if you are taking a computer or written test and practice (and strategize) accordingly! Neither the SAT nor PSAT are currently offered as CAT tests.

Essay
Tests: Write on!

S ome students love essays, some hate them. Personally, I think *all* "objective" tests are harder than essay tests. Why? An objective test of any kind gives the teacher much more latitude to concentrate on specifics, even the option of focusing *only* on the most obscure details (which, granted, only the truly sadistic would do). As a result, it's much more difficult to eliminate areas or topics when studying for such a test. It's also rare to be given a choice—answer 25 out of 50—whereas you may often be given, for example, five essay questions and have to choose only three. This greatly increases the odds that even sporadic studying will have given you *some* grasp of one or two of the questions, whereas you may be lost on a 100-question true/false test.

Whether you love or hate essays, there are some important pointers to ensure that you at least score better on them.

THINK BEFORE YOU INK

You need to budget your time for an essay test just as you should for any test—the mathematical calculations are just easier. Five questions in 50 minutes? Doesn't take an Einstein to figure out 10 minutes per essay.

Or does it? In this example, allow 7 or 8 minutes per essay, which will give you anywhere from 10 to 15 minutes to review, proofread, and make corrections and additions to all your answers. And if any of the questions are "weighted" more than the others, adjust the time you spend on them accordingly.

When the time you've budgeted for the first question is up, immediately move on to the next, no matter how far you've gotten on the first. You'll have time at the end—if you follow my suggestion—to go back and add more. *Most teachers will give you a better overall grade for five incomplete but decent essays than for three excellent ones and two left blank.*

Don't ever, *ever* begin writing the answer to an essay question without a little "homework" first, even if you're the school's prize-winning journalist.

First, really look at the question. Are you sure you know what it's asking? Put it in your own words and compare it with your teacher's. Do they clearly mean the same thing? If not, you've misread it.

One way to avoid this problem is to make your paraphrase the first sentence of your essay. Even if you have misread the teacher's question, you have shown her how *you* interpreted it. Even if you answer a slightly different question than the teacher intended, you may get full credit for a well-written essay.

But please *don't*, intentionally or otherwise, misread the question in such a way that you answer the question you'd *like* rather than the one you've actually been given.

Make sure you understand the meaning of the "direction verbs." Don't "describe" when you've been told to "compare and contrast." Don't "explain" when you're supposed to "argue." See p. 72 for a list of the most-used such verbs and what each is instructing you to do.

A FOOLPROOF ACTION PLAN

Here's a step-by-step way to answer any essay question.

Step 1: On a blank sheet of paper, write down all the facts, ideas, concepts, and so forth, you feel should be included in your answer. (If you don't have extra paper, the back of your blue book or the test itself will work just as well.)

Step 2: Organize them in the order in which they should appear. You don't have to rewrite your notes into a detailed outline—just number each note according to where you want it in your essay.

Step 3: Compose your first paragraph. It should summarize and introduce the key points you will make in your essay. This is where superior essay answers are made or unmade.

Step 4: Write your essay, with your penmanship as legible as possible. Most teachers I've known do not attempt to decipher chicken scratch masquerading as an essay and do not award high grades to it either.

Step 5: Reread your essay and, if necessary, add points left out, correct spelling, grammar, and so on. Also watch for a careless omission that could cause serious damage—like leaving out a "not," for example, and making the point opposite the one you intended to write.

If there is a particular fact you know is important and should be included, but you just don't remember it, take a guess. Otherwise, just leave it out and do the best you can. If the rest of your essay is well thought out and organized and clearly communicates all the other points that should be included, I doubt most teachers will mark you down too severely for such an omission.

Don't set yourself up for a poor grade by making guesses you really don't have to. If you think something occurred in 1784, but are afraid it could be 1794, just write "in the late 18th century." You probably will *not* be marked down for the latter phrase, but *will* lose a point or two if you cite a wrong date.

Remember: Few teachers will be impressed by length. A well-organized, well-constructed, specific answer will always get you a better grade than "shotgunning"—writing down everything you know in the faint hope that you will actually hit something. Writing a superior essay on the little you do know will usually earn you a better grade than knowing a lot and presenting it poorly.

Start out right, with a brief, to-the-point first paragraph that doesn't meander or "pad." ("What were the similarities between Dante's Beatrice and Joyce's Molly Bloom? To truly answer this question, we must first embark upon a study of Italian and Irish literature, politics, and culture at the time...." Have we wasted enough of our precious time trying to cover up our lack of knowledge here?) End your essay with a clearly written and organized paragraph that offers more than just a summation of what you've already written.

Worry less about the specific words and more about the information. Organize your answer to a fault and write to be understood, not to impress. Better to use shorter sentences, paragraphs, and words—and be clear and concise—than let the teacher fall into a clausal nightmare from which he may never emerge (and neither will your A!).

If you don't have the faintest clue what the question means, ask. If you still don't have any idea of the answer—and I mean *zilch*—leave it blank. Writing down everything you think you know about the supposed subject in the hopes that *some*thing is pertinent is, in my mind, a waste of everyone's time. Better to allocate more time to other parts of the test and do a better job on those.

THE BEST-ORGANIZED BEATS THE BEST-WRITTEN

While I think numbering your notes is as good an organizational tool as jotting down a complete outline, there is certainly nothing wrong with fashioning a quick outline. Not one with Roman numerals—this outline will consist of a simple list of abbreviated words, scribbled on a piece of scrap paper or in the margin of your test booklet.

The purpose of this outline is the same as that of those fancy ones: to make sure you include everything you need and want to say—in order.

It's important to write well. But excellent writing, even pages and pages of it, will not get you an excellent grade unless you write quality answers—hard-hitting, incisive, and direct.

Think of the introduction and the conclusion as the bread in a sandwich, with the information in between as the hamburger, lettuce, tomato, and pickle. All of the ingredients are necessary, but the tastiest part is what's inside the bun.

GIVE ME SOME SPACE, MAN

Plan ahead. Write your essay on every other line and on one side of the paper or page only. This will give you room to add or correct anything without having to write it so small that it is illegible and, therefore, doesn't earn you any credit.

It also helps keep the whole paper neater and, psychologically, that should help you get a slightly better grade. Most teachers won't admit it, but they will give a few more points to tests that are neat, clean, and done with a good pen. Think about it. How many slobs do you know who are A students?

PROOF IT!

Budget your time so that you can go back over your essay, slowly, and correct any mistakes or make any additions. Check your spelling, punctuation, grammar, and syntax. (If you don't know what syntax is, find out. You'll need to know for the SAT.) It would be a shame for you to write a beautiful, thorough essay and lose points because of careless errors.

WHEN YOU'RE DONE, YOU'RE DONE...ALMOST

Resist the temptation to leave the room or turn in your paper before you absolutely must. Imagine the pain of sitting in the cafeteria, while everyone else is still working on the test, and suddenly remembering what else you could have said to make your essay really sparkle. Sorry. Too late!

Take the time at the end of the test to review not only your essay answers, but your other answers as well. Make sure all words and numbers are readable. Make sure you have matched the right question and the right answer. Even make sure you didn't miss a whole section by turning over a page too quickly or not noticing that a page was missing. Make sure you can't, simply *can't*, add anything more to any of the essay answers.

IF YOU'RE OUT OF TIME, ARE YOU OUT OF LUCK?

While you should have carefully allocated sufficient time to complete each essay before you started working on the first, things happen. You may find yourself with two minutes left and one full essay to go. What do you do? As quickly as possible, write down every piece of information you think should be included in your answer, and number each point in the order in which you would have written it. If you then have time to reorganize your notes into a better-organized outline, do so. Many teachers will give you at least partial credit (some very near full credit) if your outline contains all the information the answer was supposed to. It will at least show you knew a lot about the subject and were capable of outlining a reasonable response.

One of the reasons you may have left yourself with insufficient time to answer one or more questions is you knew too darned much about the previous question(s), and you wanted to make sure the teacher knew you knew, so you wrote…and wrote…and wrote…until you ran out of time.

Be careful—some teachers throw in a relatively general question that, if you wanted to, you could write about until next Wednesday. In that case, they aren't testing your knowledge of the whole subject as much as your ability to edit yourself, to organize and summarize the important points.

Just remember that no matter how fantastic your answer to any one essay, it is going to get one-fifth the overall score (presuming 5 questions)—that is, 20 points, never more, even if you turn in a publishable book manuscript. Meanwhile, 80 points are unclaimed.

If you've mastered the tips and techniques in this chapter, you will, from now on, "be like Ron": You'll positively drool when you see a test that's nothing but essays!

COMMON INSTRUCTIONAL VERBS ON ESSAY TESTS

Compare
Examine two or more objects, ideas, people, etc., and note similarities and differences.

Contrast
Compare to highlight differences. Similar to differentiate, distinguish.

Criticize
Judge and discuss merits and faults. Similar to critique.

Define
Explain the nature or essential qualities.

Describe
Convey appearance, nature, attributes, etc.

Discuss
Consider or examine by argument, comment, etc.; debate; explore solutions.

Enumerate
List various events, things, descriptions, ideas, etc.

Evaluate
Appraise the worth of an idea, comment, etc., and justify your conclusion.

Explain
Make the meaning of somethingclear, plain, intelligible, and/or understandable.

Illustrate
Use specific examples or analogies to explain.

Interpret
Give the meaning of something by paraphrase, by translation, or by an explanation based on personal opinion.

Justify   Defend a statement or conclusion. Similar to support.

Narrate   Recount the occurrence of something, usually by giving details of events in the order in which they occurred. Similar to describe, but only applicable to something that happens in time.

Outline   Do a general sketch, account, or report, indicating only the main features of a book, subject, or project.

Prove   Establish the truth or genuineness by evidence or argument. Similar to show, explain why, demonstrate. (In math, verify validity by mathematical demonstration.)

Relate   Give an account of events and/or circumstances, usually to establish association, connections, or relationships.

Review   Survey a topic, occurrence, or idea, generally but critically. Similar to describe, discuss, illustrate, outline, summarize, trace. Some test makers may use these words virtually interchangeably, although one can find subtle differences in each.

State   Present the facts concisely and clearly. May be used interchangeably with name, list, indicate, identify, enumerate, cite.

Summarize   State in concise form, omitting examples and details.

Trace   Follow the course or history of an occurrence, idea, etc.

Objective Tests: Discriminate and Eliminate

●●●

Some people prefer objective tests to essays. After all, in multiple-choice questions, the answer is staring you in the face (and secretly sticking out its tongue at you, if you don't recognize it). You just have to be able to figure out which one it is.

In this chapter, we're going to look at the different types of objective questions and some of the methods you can use to answer them, based primarily on "the process of elimination."

If you learn nothing else from this chapter, learn this: The process of elimination has saved many a person from failure. It may just save you.

ANSWER EVERY *OTHER* QUESTION? ARRRGGHHH!

A very key point of preparation for *any* kind of test: Read and understand the directions. And *listen* to any last-minute instructions from your teacher. Otherwise, you could seemingly do everything *right*, but not follow his explicit directions, in which case everything's going to be *wrong*.

If you're supposed to check off *every* correct answer to each question in a multiple choice test—and you're assuming only *one* answer to each question is correct—you're going to miss a lot of answers and lose a lot of points!

If you're to pick one essay question out of three, or two out of five, you will almost certainly run out of time if you try to answer every one. Even if you do manage to complete all five, the teacher will probably only grade the first two. Because you allocated so much time to the other three, it's highly doubtful your first two answers will be detailed and polished enough to earn a good grade.

In the case of a standardized test, such as the SAT or GRE, read the instructions from a previous test *before* you go to the test site. (There are numerous books that include "actual tests" in their prep books, and practice tests can be downloaded from many Web sites.) Then just skim the instructions in your booklet or on the computer to make sure nothing has changed. It will save you minutes, time that is precious indeed during any such test.

Are the questions or sections weighted? Some tests may have two, three, or more sections, some of which count for very little—10 or 15 percent of your final score. One part, usually a major essay, may be more heavily weighted—50 percent or more of your grade. Let this influence the amount of time and energy you devote to each section.

Beware of time. Again, if questions or sections are weighted, you will want to allow extra time for those that count for 90 percent of the score and whip through the 10 percent section as the teacher is collecting booklets.

I know students who look through the entire test and break it down into time segments before they read any question or write a single answer—allocating 20 minutes for section one, 40 for section two, and so forth. Even on multiple choice tests, they count the total number of questions, divide by the time allotted, and set "goals" on what time they should reach question 10, question 25, and so on.

I never did it, but I think it's a great idea—if it turns out to be a workable organizational tool for you and not just one more layer of pressure.

If there are pertinent facts or formulas you're afraid you'll forget, I think it's a good idea to write them down somewhere in your test booklet before you do anything else. It won't take much time, and it could save some serious memory jogs later.

When a guess isn't just a guess

Will you be penalized for guessing? The teacher may inform you that you will earn two points for every correct answer, but *lose* one point for every incorrect one. This will certainly affect whether you guess or skip the question—or, at the very least, how many potential answers you feel you need to eliminate before the odds of guessing are in your favor. As far as the SAT is concerned, there isn't a penalty for guessing, so don't leave an answer blank!

There is usually nothing wrong with guessing, unless, of course, you know wrong answers will be penalized.

Even then, the question is how *often* to guess (and on what basis).

If there's no penalty for wrong answers, you should *never* leave an answer blank. But you should also do everything you can to increase your odds of getting it right. If every multiple-choice question gives you four possible answers, you have a 25 percent chance of being right (and, of course, a 75 percent chance of being wrong) each time you have to guess.

But if you can eliminate a single answer—one you are reasonably certain cannot be right—your chances of being correct increase to 33 percent.

And, of course, if you can get down to a choice between two answers, it's just like flipping a coin: 50-50. In the long run, you will guess as many right as wrong.

Even if there is a penalty for guessing, I would probably pick one answer if I had managed to reduce the odds to 50-50.

Presuming that you've managed to eliminate one or more answers but are still unsure of the correct answer and have no particular way to eliminate any others, here are some real insider tips to make your "guess" more educated:

○ If two answers sound alike, choose neither.

○ The most "obvious" answer to a difficult question is probably wrong, but an answer that is close to it is probably right.

○ If the answers that are left to a mathematical question cover a broad range, eliminate the extremes and choose a number in the middle.

○ If two quantities are very close, choose one of them.

○ If two numbers differ only by a decimal point (and the others aren't close), choose one of them.

(Example: 2.3, 40, 1.5, 6, 15; I'd go with 1.5 or 15. If I could at least figure out from the question where the decimal point should go, even better!)

○ If two answers to a mathematical problem look alike —either formulas or shapes—choose one of them.

Remember: This is not the way to ace a test—these are just some tried-and-true ways to increase your guessing power when *you have absolutely nothing else to go on and nothing left to do.*

ELIMINATE THE OBVIOUS AND SORT OF OBVIOUS

Suppose the question was as follows: "The first U.S. President to appoint a woman to the Cabinet was (A) Franklin D. Roosevelt, (B) Herbert Hoover, (C) Abraham Lincoln, or (D) Jimmy Carter."

"Heck if I know," you may be saying to yourself. Most likely, you can get the answer down to two choices pretty quickly. Why is that? Think for a moment about women's rights and the role of women in American society. Okay, that's long enough.

You're absolutely correct to eliminate, right away, Abraham Lincoln. It wasn't that he was a bad guy; you just have to remember that women didn't even have the right to vote at that time, and laws and customs kept women from doing most of what they are doing today. The like- lihood of a woman being in the President's Cabinet in the 1860s is very, very, very slim.

Let's now go to the other extreme. You may be fuzzy on who was in Jimmy Carter's Cabinet (he may have been fuzzy, too), but even if you are too young to remember Carter, you're guessing that he was recent enough not to be the *first* president to appoint women in that role. Score another point for the process of elimination.

Now comes the hard part. If you have any knowledge of history, and I hope you do, you know that the two remaining choices were, at least, presidents during the 20th century...in other words, after women were granted the right to vote.

You may not know enough to make even an educated guess. But even if you blindly select one of the two, you have even odds of being right. Even if your teacher deducts points for wrong answers, I would go ahead and put down (A) or (B).

Those of you who know a little more about history are going to remember that Roosevelt was controversial because of his dramatic restructuring of the government, while Hoover was the poster boy for the Status Quo Society. If that difference in their styles and actions comes to mind, then you'd be correct in choosing FDR.

CHECK IT OUT, CHECK IT OUT!

Use this process of elimination for all types of objective questions. Depending on whether you can eliminate any of the answers and whether you feel you can "afford" to lose the points will help you decide how to answer the question.

If there is time during a test for you to come back to questions and think about them one more time, go ahead and cross out the answers you know aren't correct. That will simply save you time. You will ignore the answers that are struck out and concentrate on the ones that remain. A small point, but it can save you several seconds per question.

What if you eliminate four out of five answers and are convinced the one that's left—your "right" answer—is definitely wrong? Eliminate *it* and start your process of elimination all over again with the other four.

Should you go back, recheck your work, and change a guess? How valid was that first guess? It was probably pretty darn good (presuming you had some basis for guessing in the first place). So good that you should *only* change it *if*:

- It really was just a wild guess and, upon further thought, you conclude that answer actually should be eliminated (in which case your next guess is, at least, not quite so wild).
- You remembered something that changed the odds of your guess completely (or the answer to a later question helped you figure out the answer to this one!).
- You miscalculated on a math problem.
- You misread the question and didn't notice a "not," "always," or other important qualifier.

GET VISUAL

Throughout a test, don't miss an opportunity to draw a picture for yourself if it helps you understand the question or figure out the right answer. If the question deals with any sort of cause-and-effect that has several steps in it, literally draw or write down those steps very quickly, using abbreviated words or symbols. This may help you see missing pieces, understand relationships between parts, and select the right answer.

18 TIPS FOR "ACING" MULTIPLE-CHOICE TESTS

1. Read the question in full before you look at any of the answers. Come up with your own answer before examining any of the choices.

2. Be careful you don't read too much into questions. Don't try to second guess the test preparer and look for patterns or tricks that aren't really there.

3. Underline the key words in a reading selection.

4. A positive choice is more likely to be correct than a negative one.

5. If two choices are very similar, the answer is probably not either one of them.

6. If two choices are opposite, one of them is probably correct.

7. Don't go against your first impulse unless you are *sure* you were wrong. (Sometimes you're so smart you scare yourself.)

8. Check for negatives and other words that are there to throw you off. ("Which of the following is not....")

9. The answer is usually *wrong* if it contains "all," "always," "never," or "none." I repeat, usually.

10. The answer has a great chance of being *right* if it has "sometimes," "probably," or "some."

11. When you don't know the right answer, seek out the wrong ones.

12. Don't eliminate an answer unless you actually know what every word means.

13. Don't seek out answer patterns. Just because answer "C" has appeared three times in a row doesn't mean "C" isn't the correct answer to the fourth question. Trust your knowledge.

14. Read every answer before you pick one. A sneaky test maker will place a decoy answer that's *almost* right first, tempting you before you've even considered the other choices.

15. On a standardized test, consider transferring all answers from one section to the answer sheet at the same time. This can save time. Just be careful: Make sure you're putting each answer in the right place.

16. The longest and/or most complicated answer to a question is often correct—the test maker has been forced to add qualifying clauses or phrases to make that answer complete and unequivocal.

17. Be suspicious of choices that seem obvious to a two-year-old. Why would the teacher give you such a gimme? Maybe she's not, that trickster!

18. Don't give up on a question that, after one reading, seems hopelessly confusing or hard. Looking at it from another angle, restating it in your own words, or drawing a picture may help you understand it after all.

ANALOGIES: STUDY:SUCCEED AS EAT:LIVE

I may be a sick puppy, but I like analogies. In the heat of completing 30 of them on a test, I may have slight second thoughts, but I look upon them as incredible brain teasers. To help you figure out the right answer in an analogy, write it out or, at least, *think* it out. Suppose the question was:

TIRED: SLEEP

(A)   athletic: swim

(B)   happy: wedding

(C)   hungry: eat

(D)   cold: blanket

What's the relationship between "tired" and "sleep"? First of all, what parts of speech are "tired" and "sleep" in this example? Adjective: verb.

The correct answer is going to have the same relationship. Two of the answers, (B) and (D), are adjective: noun. So you've eliminated two of the four already.

What is the relationship between "tired" and "sleep"? "Sleep" is something you do when you are "tired."

Now which choice seems correct, A or C? If you substitute "hungry" and "eat" in the above sentence, doesn't it sound correct? But if you put "athletic" and "swim" in the same places, does it make sense? Not really. Certainly people who are athletic swim, but many athletes do not, and many people who aren't athletes may swim.

SOME SAMPLES FOR YOU TO TASTE

Many of these basic principles apply to the other types of questions you'll find on an objective test. Matching one item with another, completing sentences, doing math problems, choosing the correct vocabulary word—they all rely on:

1. Your prior knowledge gained from studying for this particular course.
2. All the reading, studying, and listening you've been doing for years.
3. Your common sense.
4. Your ability to eliminate as many as possible of the potential answers.
5. Following directions.

COMPREHENSION QUESTIONS

This is the portion of the test where you find a short essay, followed by several questions. You are supposed to find the answers to those questions in the essay. Unlike the multiple-choice questions, where the answer is actually right in front of you, the answers to the essay questions may well be hidden in one fashion or another.

Not since third grade have you had an essay question that asks, "How old was John F. Kennedy when he married Jacqueline Bouvier?" and, lo and behold, back in the essay it clearly says, "John F. Kennedy was 36 years old when he married Jacqueline Bouvier." Unfortunately for you, those questions disappeared around the same time as notes that said, "Do you love me? Yes or No!" and recess.

You're lucky if you get questions like, "How old was John F. Kennedy when he was elected president?" and the essay says, "John F. Kennedy took office 21 years after graduating *cum laude* from Harvard in 1940."

Buried somewhere else in the essay will be something like, "Kennedy was born in 1917, the second of nine children of Joseph and Rose Kennedy." Since you should know that Kennedy took office in 1961, you can figure out that he was 43 years old when he was elected in 1960. The rest is history.

Here's the method I recommend for answering comprehension questions:

1. Read the questions before you read the selection. They will alert you to what you're looking for and affect the way you read the passage. If dates are asked for, circle all dates in the passage as you read. If you're looking for facts rather than conclusions, it will, again, change the way you read the passage.

2. When you first read the question, before you look at the answers, decide what you *think* the answer is. If your answer is one of the choices, bingo!

3. Slowly read the essay, keeping in mind the questions you've just read. Don't underline too much, but do underline conjunctions that alter the direction of the sentence: "however," "although," "nevertheless," "yet," and so forth. Because of this shift, there is a good chance that this sentence will figure in one of the questions.

   For example: "John Smith was the kind of writer who preferred writing over editing, *while* his wife Lois was interested in the latter over the former," might provide the answer to the question: "Did Lois Smith prefer writing or editing?" A careless glance back at the text will cause you to select "writing" as the answer.

4. Read the questions again. Then go back and forth, finding out the answer to the first one, the second one, and so forth. Don't skip around unless the first question is an absolute stumper. If you jump around too much, you'll get confused again and you won't answer any of the questions very completely or even correctly.

You're Failing This Test: True or False?

I think true/false tests are generally more insidious than multiple-choice. But it's awfully hard to ask for better than 50-50 odds!

What can you do to increase your scores on true-false tests? Be more inclined to guess if you have to. After all, I encouraged you to guess on a multiple-choice test if you could eliminate enough wrong answers to get down to two, one of which is correct. Well, you're already there! So, unless you are being penalized for guessing, guess away! Even if you are being penalized, you may want to take a shot if you have the faintest clue of the correct answer.

In fact, your odds are often better than 50-50. Most test preparers tend to include more "true" statements than false. So if you really don't have any way to determine the truth of a statement, *presume it is true*. If there is a specific detail in the statement—"There are 206 bones in the adult human body"—it may also tend to be true.

Remember: For a statement to be true, every part of that statement must be true. Be careful of statements whose parts *are* true (or at least *may* be true), linked in such a way that the *whole* statement becomes false. Example: "Since many birds can fly, they use stones to grind their food." Many birds *do* fly, and birds *do* swallow stones to grind their food. But a *causal relationship* (the word "since") between the two clauses makes the *whole* statement false.

The longer and/or more complicated a statement in a true/false test, the less likely it's true since every clause of it must be true (and there are so many chances for a single part of it to be false).

Be careful of double negatives: A statement claiming that something is "not uncommon" actually means that it is common.

Few broad, general statements are true *without exception*. So always be on your guard when you see the words "all," "always," "no," "never," "everyone," "best," "worst," "none," "nobody," or other absolutes. As long as you can think of a *single* example which proves such a statement false, then it's false. But be wary: There are statements containing such absolutes that *are* true; they are just rare. "All U.S. presidents (and/or vice presidents) have been men" is, unfortunately, all too true.

Likewise, words like "sometimes," "often," "frequently," "generally," "usually," "much," "may," "probably," "might," and "ordinarily" make more modest claims and thus usually indicate "true" statements.

Strategy tip: It's easier for a teacher to add something that makes a statement false than the other way around. So when you read it, look for anything that will make the whole statement false. If you can't find it, assume it is true.

MATCHING

Match the following countries with their capitals:

Berlin	Chile
Athens	China
Santiago	Greece
Beijing	Germany

Match the obvious ones first. Let's say you know Berlin and Beijing are the capitals of Germany and China, respectively. Look at the two remaining choices. Here is where common sense and good general knowledge come in handy.

Because you probably get a lot of your world news from the radio and TV, you may well have heard the combos more than you've seen them. Go with the ones that "sound right." (In this case, Athens, Greece, and Santiago, Chile.)

Wait to guess in matching questions until you have gone through both lists at least once and have answered all the ones you are sure of. Guessing too early will often eliminate an answer you need later.

SENTENCE COMPLETIONS

Like many of the other kinds of problems, sentence completions can often be figured out by putting the question into context or into perspective. It's especially important to focus on how the sentence is written. Here's an example:

> The clerk at the clothing boutique asked the woman, "What's your ___?"
>
> (A)   age
> (B)   size
> (C)   color
> (D)   religion

Of course a sales clerk could ask her customers about their ages, colors, and religions, but in a clothing boutique, asking a customer's size makes the most sense.

Presuming this type of test is assessing your mastery of a particular vocabulary list, provide a descriptive answer if you're unable to recall an exact word. Some teachers will give partial credit.

MULTIPLE-CHOICE MATH

Process of elimination can save you immense amounts of time and calculation. For example, scan the problem below and see if you can figure out the answer *without actually doing the math*:

$$334 \times 412 =$$
(A)   54,559
(B)   137,608
(C)   22,528
(D)   229,766

By performing one simple calculation, you can eliminate two of the choices. Multiply the last digits in the two numbers (2×4). The answer must end in 8! So (A) and (D) have been eliminated...that fast!

Now, eyeball (B) and (C). Can you find the right answer quickly? This is *educated* guessing, known in math circles as "guesstimating." Look: 334×100 is 33,400, so 334×412 *must* be greater than 33,400. (C) *has* to be wrong. (B) is the answer, by process of elimination.

Should you do the actual math to double check your answer? I wouldn't. You are *certain* that (A) and (D) are wrong. You *know* that (C) is much too low. Mark (B) as the answer and move on.

Here are other ways to better your score on math tests:

○ Try to figure out what is being asked, what principles are involved, what information is important, and what's not. Don't let extraneous data throw you off track. Make sure you know the *kind* of answer you're seeking: Is it a speed, weight, angle, exponent, square root?

o Whenever you can, "translate" formulas and numbers into words. Estimate the answer before you even begin the actual calculation. At least you'll know the size of the ballpark you're playing in!

o Even if you're not particularly visual, pictures can often help. Try translating a particularly vexing math problem into a drawing or diagram.

o Play around. There are often different paths to the same solution, or even equally valid solutions.

o When you are checking your calculations, try working *backwards*. I've found it an easier way to catch simple arithmetical errors.

o Try to write down all of your calculations—neatly. You'll be less likely to make a mistake if you take your time, and if you *do* make a mistake, it will be a lot easier to spot.

o Show every step and formula, even if you would normally skip a few. If you knew all of the principles and formulas but miscalculated near the very beginning of your analysis, you are not going to arrive at the correct answer. *But* many enlightened math teachers will take very little off if they can clearly see you knew your stuff and managed to do everything right, with the exception of hitting the right button on your calculator.

o And if you're using a calculator, double check your answer immediately. The chances of hitting a wrong number are high; the chances of hitting the same wrong number are not.

THE IMPORTANCE OF WORDS

No matter how much you study principles and examples, you will be lost if the words used in the test are simply not in your vocabulary. I could make the point, of course, that without a sufficient vocabulary, you won't be able to keep up with the principles anyway. Like reading itself, building a workable vocabulary is absolutely essential to doing well on any kind of test, since you are more likely to understand the directions, the questions, and the possible answers.

Build your vocabulary as much as you can. Read good books. Listen to people who have large vocabularies. Write down words you don't know and become familiar with them. The more words you know, the better you can play the elimination game and the better score you'll get. I highly recommend *Better Vocabulary in 30 Minutes a Day* by Edie Schwager (Career Press, 1996), for those of you who are word challenged.

ALL OF THE ABOVE, NONE OF THE ABOVE

Some teachers have fallen in love with "all of the above" and "none of the above." You can't take one of their tests without those phrases appearing in every other question.

"All of the above" is often the right answer if it is an option. *Hope* that you see it as a potential answer to *every* question because *it gives you a much better chance to do better on the test* than your mastery of the material (or lack thereof) might normally warrant. Why? Because you don't have to be really sure that "all of the above" is correct to choose it. All you have to be is *pretty* sure that *two* answers are correct (and equally sure the others are not *necessarily* wrong). As long as you believe there is more than one correct answer, then "all of the above" *must* be the right choice!

Likewise, you don't have to be convinced that "none of the above" is the right answer, just *reasonably* sure that none of the other answers are absolutely correct.

Just be careful to read those instructions! If they say, "Choose the *best* answer" and you rapidly choose "(A) the Andes," you lose if (A) is merely *a* correct answer. "(E) all of the above" will still be the *best* answer if every *other* answer is *also* correct.

Here's a sample analysis to show you why you should love teachers infatuated with "all" and "none":

> Which of the following authors won the Nobel Prize for Literature in the 1990s?
>
> (A)   Gunter Grass
>
> (B)   Toni Morrison
>
> (C)   Seamus Heaney
>
> (D)   All of the above
>
> (E)   None of the above

Do you know for a fact that one of them *didn't* win? Yes? Then you *eliminate* (D) as a possibility. Do you know whether *any* of them won? If so, you eliminate (E). Do you know if *two* of them won? Let's say you know that Toni Morrison was a winner in 1993 and that Gunter Grass won in 1999, but you've never even heard of Seamus Heaney. *Doesn't matter*—once you know *two* won, (D) is the *only* possible answer.

A WORD ABOUT "EASY" TESTS

Some people think "open-book" tests are the easiest of all. They pray for them...at least until they see their first one.

These are the toughest tests of all, if only because even normally "nice" teachers feel no compunction whatsoever about making such tests as tough as a Marine drill instructor. *Heck, you can use your book!* That's like having a legal crib sheet, right? Worse yet, many open-book tests are also take-home tests, meaning you can use your notes (and any other books or tools you can think of).

Since you have to anticipate that there will be no easy questions, no matter how well you know that material, you need to do some preparation before you deal with this type of test.

- Mark important pages by turning down corners, using paper clips, or any other method that will help you quickly flip to important charts, tables, summaries, or illustrations.
- Write an index of the pages you've turned down so you know where to look immediately for a specific chart, graph, table, and so forth.
- Summarize all important facts, formulas, etc., on a separate sheet.
- If you are also allowed to bring your notes or it's a take-home test, write a brief index to your notes (general topics only) so you know where to find pertinent information.

Answer the questions you don't need the book for first, including those of which you're fairly sure and know where to check the answers in your book. Star the latter ones.

Then use the book. Check starred answers first and erase the stars once you have completed them. Then work on those questions on which you must rely fully on the book.

Be careful about quoting too freely from your text. Better to make up a similar example than use the same one in your book. Better to paraphrase your text than quote it directly, even if you use quotation marks.

While a take-home test is, by definition, an open-book test, it is the hardest of all. An open-book test in class simply can't last longer than the time allotted for the class. You may be given a night or two, or even a week or longer, to complete a take-home exam.

Why are they so hard? You're *given* so much time because teachers expect that it will take you *longer* than the time available in class to finish. You may have to go well beyond your text(s) and notes even to get a handle on some of the questions, leading to some long nights. Take any *easy* eight-hour tests lately? The longer you're given, the easier it is to procrastinate ("Heck, I've got another two nights!"), and we know where *that* leads.

There are only two good aspects to balance the scales. You've certainly been given the chance to "be all that you can be." No excuse for not doing a terrific job on a test with virtually no time limit. If you tend to freeze during a normal exam, you should have far less anxiety at home in comfortable surroundings.

CHAPTER

SEVEN

Psyching up on Exam Day

"IT IS NOT ENOUGH TO SUCCEED. OTHERS MUST FAIL."
—GORE VIDAL

● ● ●

W ell, here you are. No longer are you thinking of the exam as being next month or next week or even tomorrow. You're sitting in the very room in the very chair and someone is heading your way with a test paper.

Are you ready? I hope you brought everything you need.

I used to make up what I called the Test Kit. Into my backpack went some pens or pencils (depending on what I needed for the test)—two or three of each; the book and workbooks associated with the test; my notes; a calculator, if allowed; a candy bar or other treat that would give me energy; photo ID; and an entry card, if required.

By collecting all this mess in one place, I wouldn't be very likely to forget it. Also, if I did something dreadful like oversleep, I only had to grab the one thing that I had packed the night before and dash out the door.

You have enough to worry about on the morning of a big test. Don't spend frantic minutes looking for something that you could have placed inside a backpack, briefcase, or large purse the night before. Be kind to yourself.

DOUBLE YOUR PLEASURE—SIT ALONE

Unless you are already in an assigned seat, try to sit near the front so you will get the exam first and have some precious seconds at the end while the other papers are being passed to the front. It also places you near the teacher or proctor for easier access for questions.

Avoid sitting near someone who has a lot of noisy jewelry, who is cracking or popping gum, or who is too friendly with the others in the immediate area. Be a hermit, in other words. Choose a quiet area.

Wear loose, comfortable clothes, the kind that you love—your favorite shirt or sweater or slacks. If you're left handed, look for a left-handed desk. Check out the room for sunlight (too much or too little), lighting, and temperature.

THE HOOSIER MEASURING SYSTEM

Remember in the movie *Hoosiers* when the team that Gene Hackman was coaching made it to the state finals? The boys walked into the fieldhouse and were overwhelmed by its size; it sure wasn't like the little gymnasiums they were used to playing in.

Coach was smart. He had them measure the basketball court. Whaddya know? It was exactly the same size as the one back in little Hickory. Point made. Point taken. They won, of course. (Oh, sorry, I thought you had seen the movie.) Pull a Gene Hackman move. Take a "measure" of the exam in front of you before you begin.

Go all the way

Begin at the beginning. Then move through to the end. No, I'm not talking about taking the exam, I'm talking about looking through the booklet or taking a glance at all the questions. If you have permission to go all the way through it, do that before you ever start. Just give yourself an overview of what lies ahead. That way you can spot the easier sections (and do them first) and get an idea of the point values assigned to each section.

You can also make sure your test is complete. Wouldn't it feel terrible to flash through the test, check your answers with minutes to spare, and *then* discover you missed that last essay question...the one that counts for 50 percent of your grade?

The art of war

There are three ways to attack a multiple-choice test:

1. Start at the first question and keep going until you reach the end, never leaving a question until you have either answered it fully or made an educated guess.

2. Answer the *easy* questions first—the ones you know the answers to without any thinking at all or those requiring the simplest calculations—then go back and do the harder ones.

3. Answer the *hardest* questions first, then go back and do the easy ones.

None of these three options is inherently right or wrong. Each may work for different individuals. (I'm assuming that these three approaches are all in the context of the test format. Weighted sections may well affect your strategy.)

The first approach is, in one sense, the quickest, in that no time is wasted reading through the whole test trying to pick out either the easiest or hardest questions. Presuming that you do not permit yourself to get stumped by a single question so you spend an inordinate amount of time on it, it is probably the method most of you usually employ.

Remember, though, to leave questions that confuse you from the outset for the end and allocate enough time to both go back to those you haven't answered and check *all* your answers thoroughly.

The second approach ensures that you will maximize your right answers—you're putting off those that you find particularly vexing.

Many experts recommend this method because they maintain that answering so many questions one after another gives you immediate confidence to tackle the questions you're not sure about. If you find that you agree, then by all means use this strategy. However, you may consider just *noting* the easy ones as you proofread the test. This takes less time and, to me, delivers the same "confidence boost."

The last approach is actually the one I used. In fact, I made it a point to do the very hardest questions first, then work my way "down" the difficulty ladder. (This means I often worked *backwards*, because many test makers and teachers make their tests progressively more difficult.)

It may sound like a strange strategy to you, so let me explain the psychology.

First of all, I figured if time pressure started getting to me near the end of the test, I would rather be in a position to answer the easiest questions—and lots of them—in the limited time left than ones I really had to think about. After all, by the end of the test, my mind was usually not working as well as at the beginning!

That's the major benefit of the third approach: When I was most "up," most awake, most alert, I tackled the questions that required the most analysis, thinking, and interpretation. When I was most tired—near the end—I was answering the questions that were virtually "gimmes."

At the same time, I was also giving myself a *real* shot of confidence. As soon as I finished the first hard question, I already felt better. When I finished all of the hard ones, everything was downhill.

I would always, however, try to ensure adequate time to at least put down an answer for every question. Better to get one question wrong and complete three other answers than to get one right and leave three blank.

It is not the approach for everybody, but it may be right for you.

And don't fall into the "answer daze," that blank stare some students get when they can't think of an answer—for 10 minutes.

Do *some*thing. Better to move on and get that one question wrong than waste invaluable time doing nothing.

Ask questions immediately if you don't understand something. The proctor may not be able to say anything (or may not know anything to say), but it's worth a try.

If you get part of a question answered and you need to return to finish it, work out a little code for yourself. Put a symbol in the margin beside the problem that means "You're partly done here—come back to this one after you've done all the ones you can do."

GUESS AND GUESS AGAIN?

If you do guess at any of the objective questions and you are getting your test paper returned to you, place a little dot or other symbol beside them. That way you will know how successful your guessing was. For example, suppose you guessed at 30 questions and got 22 of them right. That tells me your guesses are, for the most part, *educated* guesses, not wild stabs in the dark, and that you earned enough points to make it worthwhile, *even if you got penalized for missing eight others*. However, if you only got six right, review my comments on educated guessing. Something's not working right for you.

When you think you have finished with a whole section, double check to see if that's true. Look on the answer sheet or in the blue book to make sure all the questions have been answered.

IT'S A LONG RACE—PACE YOURSELF

If you have 100 multiple-choice questions and you have 50 minutes allotted for that section, you don't have to be MIT material to figure that you should spend a maximum of 30 seconds on each answer. Check your progress two or three times during the 50 minutes.

Which reminds me: Don't depend on a wall clock to tell you the time. Bring your watch. Some students like to remove it and place it on the desk so they can see it without having to look down at their wrist, especially if the writing hand and the watch hand are different.

For COMPUTER-SCORED TESTS

If you are required to color in a little rectangle to show which answer is correct so that a machine can score the results, mark the answer sheet very carefully. Stray pencil marks can be picked up by the computer, causing the wrong answer to be recorded. If you carefully filled in one box, only to change your mind later, completely, *completely* erase the first answer. If the computer picks up both markings, guess what happens? You don't get the point, even if one of the boxes is correct.

You DESERVE A BREAK TODAY

Take the breaks that are offered. You'll benefit in the long run by going to the bathroom, getting a drink of water, eating a candy bar, or all of the above, rather than sitting there working through another algebraic equation.

Just as you needed the good sleep you got during the week, you'll need to be energized by the breaks. Besides, suppose you didn't move, and then, 20 minutes after the break, you've got to go the bathroom. Desperately. What if the proctor won't let you? Do you kill him and take the SAT while in prison at West Bubba, Arkansas? Or do you act smart and take the break when everyone else does?

You DON'T NEED A GYM TO EXERCISE

You can perform some unobtrusive exercises at your desk that will make you feel refreshed. Try them right now. First, tense up your feet—squeeze them hard, then relax them, then squeeze them. Then do the same with the muscles in your calves, shoulders, hips and abdomen. It's a pretty simple exercise, but I find it energizes me when I am unable to get up and move around the room. Even moving the facial muscles helps. Do them looking down at your paper; otherwise your teacher will think you are having a coronary or making faces at her.

If there is time at the end of the test, review. Go back and check over answers to essay questions that may not be as complete as you'd like them to be, or look again at the unanswered questions in any other section.

If you have even more time, look at the "guess" questions you've marked. Does anything suddenly make sense, making you change your mind? Remember what I said about going with your first choice, but if you suddenly remember that the Catskills are in New York and not in North Dakota, change the answer!

FOR MY NEXT TRICK

If you've just finished a big, big test, get out of town. Go to a movie or a party or something that will allow you to forget, for a few hours, that you have been keeping your nose to the grindstone for the past several days.

Go. Relax. Then read Chapter 8.

Post-test Survival and Review

"WINNING ISN'T EVERYTHING, BUT WANTING TO WIN IS."
—VINCE LOMBARDI

Wanting to win *is* important. Otherwise, why would you study so hard and give up so much for so long?

Now that you've done the studying and taken the test, you want to know the results.

Let's assume you did well. Congratulations! But, no matter how many points you earned, reviewing the test is a vitally important exercise in preparing yourself for the next test—and for taking a hard look at the way you study.

If you take a standardized test and have the chance to get a copy of the exam—and your own answers—do so. It may cost you a few bucks, but I definitely think it's worth it. It's unlikely you'll find they made any mistakes in the scoring of the exam, but it will be good exercise for you to review what you got right and what you didn't while the test is reasonably fresh in your mind.

The emphasis in this chapter, however, is on the tests given by your teachers. Most will review the overall results of the test with the class on the day they are returned. First of all, you want to make sure the answers that you missed are truly incorrect. Teachers make mistakes. I know that comes as a shock.

Don't become a nuisance by challenging everything in class, waving your hand and saying, in a pleading voice, "But, but, Mr. Squeezicks! I meant to say George Washington Carver instead of George Washington!" My daughter Lindsay has become somewhat notorious for always claiming to have known all the answers, making it difficult for her to explain why she got 5 or 10 or more marked wrong!

Concentrate on the answers that are clearly marked wrong. Even a semialert student evaluating his or her own exam can grab a couple of extra points and those points might move you up another letter grade.

If the question really was ambiguous and your answer could arguably be as correct as the one the teacher chose, go ahead and make a pitch. This will be especially effective if a few others in the class chose the same answer. There *is* strength in numbers.

Your chances will be a lot better if you keep the discussion on a diplomatic level, of course, rather than getting snotty or snide. Teachers can get defensive sometimes.

Let's suppose you got the answer wrong, fair and square. Most likely, you got it wrong for one of these reasons:

YOU MADE A CARELESS MISTAKE

1. You wrote down the wrong letter or number. You knew the answer was (A), but, in your haste, you wrote down (B).

2. Similarly, you filled in the wrong box in the answer sheet. You see the mistake now. You vow not to do it again. (Good. That's the first step on the road to recovery.)

3. You left out a whole section of the test because you didn't turn the page, or you "thought" you had done it, or...

4. You wrote in such a scribbled fashion or crammed the words together so much that the teacher pulled an "I can't read it so it's wrong" deal on you and gave you no credit. (I'm on his side. Get your act—and your penmanship—together.)

5. You misread the directions. You missed the slightly important word "not," so you provided the exact opposite of what you should have.

6. You guessed wildly without even reading the options and ignored the fact that points would be deducted for wrong answers, so you got fewer points than if you had left the answer sheet blank for those questions.

YOU DIDN'T KNOW THE MATERIAL

1. You didn't read all the assignments, or get a complete set of class notes, or find out answers to questions you had about some of the information.

2. You attended class, took notes, and read the assignments, but you didn't understand what the topic was all about.

3. You needed to know a lot of facts—dates, names, events, causes, and effects—and you didn't.

YOUR PERSONAL LIFE GOT IN THE WAY

1. You brought into the test your worries that the person you're dating is going to dump you, that your parents are fighting again, or that your kids are heading to reform school if you don't do something right now.

2. You had a horrible cold, had a terrible headache, or you got too little or too much sleep.

NEXT TIME YOU'LL KNOW BETTER

Don't beat up on yourself too much. Do take time to evaluate how you did—the bad and the good. Maybe you always hated essay questions and this time you did well. It's as important to evaluate why you *were* successful as why you *weren't*.

In that case, maybe you learned a lot from your study group. Maybe your teacher gave you some good advice. Maybe you reread the pertinent sections of your textbook just before the test. Maybe you're picking up reading and comprehension skills from a combination of factors. Think back over what you may have done differently this time. Give yourself a lot of the credit. After all, you took the test all by yourself. Pat-on-the-back time!

The worrisome part is the "careless mistake" area, yet it's probably the easiest to correct, too. Take a vow that you won't do such silly things again. It's especially annoying when you knew the right answer and inadvertently circled the wrong one. Next time, pay a little closer attention to what you're doing and pace yourself so you can double check your work.

THERE'S NO SUBSTITUTE FOR KNOWLEDGE

If you go into the test knowing only half the material, don't expect to get above the 50 percent mark. Doing well on a test, as I've been telling you all along, is a combination of knowing how to take the test and knowing the stuff that goes into the answers.

If you can't seem to get prepared, maybe you'd better go back and reread the relevent earlier chapters. Get to class, get your work organized, manage your time, read the book, do your homework, the whole *shtick*.

Now's the time to see where the teacher got the questions that made up the test. What percentage of the test came from the lectures? From the book? From handouts?

It is unlikely that you're going to get an A in every class you take, but you can get the best grade possible. Even in classes that, for whatever reason, are way, way over your head, you can at least pass. In most cases, you're going to do a lot better than that.

Ask questions. Ask questions during class. Ask questions when you meet with your teacher. Join a study group and ask questions. Ask questions when the test results are being discussed.

Keep it all in perspective

What nerve you have! A personal life, you say? Isn't chemistry 104 or American government more important?

Of course not. But turn the personal motor off now and then and spend time with your friends down at the Continental Congress.

Yes, we all have colds and sore feet and heartbreaks. This is life, after all. But we can compartmentalize the parts of our life now and then without going overboard with it.

Guess how you did

Don't forget to see how many of your guesses you got right. Naturally, the better you know the material, the fewer guesses you need to make, but on some big tests you may make a lot of them.

And the door prize goes to...

After you've sacrificed to get a good grade on the exam, treat yourself. A little fun-and-games reward system is in order. Study really hard for four hours, have a candy bar. Get a B on the quiz about the French Revolution, go to a movie.

When you have something to look forward to, even though you realize it's a game (hey, life is a game, so play along!), it makes it "fun" to push yourself in order to kick back and relax.

LET'S TRY THAT ONE AGAIN

If you really messed up the test, sit down with your teacher and discuss the reasons (having done your self evaluation, based on the areas mentioned in this chapter).

Ask if you can take another test—you may not be able to get any credit for it, but you'll impress him, and he will look more kindly upon you when it comes time to assign your final grade.

Retaking "bad" tests is a good idea for another reason. Unless you just completely messed up in getting the right answers matched to the right questions, you probably performed so poorly because you didn't know the material well enough the first time.

Now you are giving yourself a second chance to learn material that will no doubt appear on future tests, and—this may come as a real shock—you might actually need to know this information for some reason in your future life.

A satisfactory completion of the retake will give you that boost of self confidence that got stomped on when you got a bad grade the first time.

But don't miss the test entirely (unless you're on your deathbed, of course) or you'll face the wrath of Mrs. Khan—the makeup exam. Think a lot of teachers look forward to creating an entirely new test *just for you*? That they're going to make it *easier* than the test you missed? Or that they'll spend *less time* with your test at home than the weekend they had to grade 30? Think you want to stay as far away from Mrs. Khan's makeup tests as Ricardo Montalban?

Good answer.

COME WITH ME NOW TO THE INNER SANCTUM

I've been talking to you about what *you* can and should do to score better on all kinds of tests. Let's take a peek in the next chapter at this whole test business from the *teacher's* point of view. C'mon, he won't bite.

How
Teachers Make up Tests

*"EXAMINATIONS ARE FORMIDABLE EVEN TO THE BEST
PREPARED, FOR THE GREATEST FOOL MAY ASK
MORE THAN THE WISEST MAN CAN ANSWER."*
—CHARLES CALEB COLTON

Apparently, Mr. Colton had just flunked his midterm. You've got one advantage over Colton: You're going to read this chapter and learn how the "greatest fools" make up those tests. I'm sorry to say that some teachers look upon tests as ways to beat down challenges to their authority ("I'll show them who knows this stuff!") or as punishment ("That'll teach them not to love English lit!"), but fortunately the key word here is "some." Let's look at how a *typical* teacher makes up a test.

I'M JUST AN AVERAGE KIND OF GUY

If students (who have studied and made a valid attempt to do well on the test) earn a grade from "excellent" to "good" to "average" (i.e., A to B to C), this tells them where they stand and the *teacher* where he stands, too.

If the test results show everyone getting an A or everyone getting Ds and Fs (after honest attempts to do well), the teacher has messed up. (The teacher may or may not recognize this, but you should.)

On tests, the majority of students will get Bs and Cs, with a small number getting As and Ds. There should be an even smaller number of Fs, "rewards" for those who truly don't have a clue or who don't care.

The test is a test of the teacher, too. The teacher has an obligation to give you information, help you understand it, make assignments that have some validity, and take you progressively through a series of learning exercises.

The test should reflect your understanding of this body of knowledge. The burden is on you to do the work and learn the material; there is an additional burden on the teacher to make sure everyone (except those who don't care) is actually learning.

The wise teacher provides several opportunities during the semester to "test" how well you are learning—quizzes (scheduled and surprise ones); papers; reports; projects; tests on units, chapters, or whole books; oral reports; and so forth. All of this should add up to your evaluation—your grade.

Some teachers love one type of question. Some are true/false freaks; others push the multiple-choice/short answer combo. If old tests, former students, the teacher's own comments on the test coming up, and your own experience tell you this is true, you might as well study for that kind of test. You still have to know the material, of course. It's just that you may need to remind yourself that you're going to have to deal with it in a particular fashion.

The best teachers use a combination of test questions to find out what you know. Frankly, some of them hate grading essay questions, so they rarely use them.

Teachers Use Essay Questions Because:

1. They are quicker and easier to prepare.
2. They may be preferred when a group is small and the test will not be reused.
3. They are used to explore students' attitudes rather than measure their achievements.
4. They are used to encourage and reward the development of the students' skill in writing.
5. They are suitable when it's important for the students to explain or describe.
6. They are more suitable to some material. You're likely to have more essay questions in English and history than you are in the sciences.

Teachers Use Objective Questions Because:

1. They are preferred when the group is large and the test may be reused.
2. They are more efficient when highly reliable test scores must be obtained quickly.
3. They are more suitable for covering a larger amount of content in the same amount of time.
4. They are easier for the teacher to give an impartial grade. Every student has to write down "C" to get number 22 correct.
5. They are easier for some teachers to create.
6. They may be used when students need to demonstrate or show.

A THOUSAND POINTS OF RIGHT

At the time the teacher decides what kinds of questions she will ask and determines what specific topics they will cover, she must also assign a point value to each question.

She will assign higher point values to questions that are concerned with material that has been emphasized in lectures, class discussions, and readings. She'll also assign more points to areas that require more time and attention.

Think about it: You've never taken a test where each true-false question was worth 20 points and the long essay was worth five. She will clearly show the points possible for each section and/or question so you can decide how to spend your time. (And if she doesn't, ask!)

TEACHERS HAVE CHECKLISTS, TOO

The teacher has selected the material to be covered. She's told you, at least in general terms, what the test will cover. She has decided on the format, assigned points, and written the questions, then double checked to make sure she has included everything she wanted to include.

She has made sure the questions are different from those on previous tests, as she suspects that some of you will look at them, hoping she'll use the same questions.

She has set up the test in a format so there is no confusion, made sure it is free of typos, and checked her questions and answers to make sure they're not ambiguous.

SHOULD WE GIVE HER A PASSING GRADE?

The "test" for her comes when she sits down to grade what you've done. If half the students completely messed up one of the questions—but messed it up in the same way—she has to admit that the directions were not clearly written. She may even decide to throw out the question.

She has determined that the number and complexity of the questions are suitable for the time allotted for the test. If she consistently finds that even her best students only completed half the test, she had too much material on the test, and, hopefully, will shorten future ones.

A key word that the teacher has to remind herself to use in making up and grading a test is "reasonable." What is a *reasonable* number of questions students can be expected to answer in 45 minutes? What should a teacher *reasonably* expect students to know from the chapters?

YOU CAN FAKE SINCERITY

No, you can't. I just said that to keep your attention. Let me leave you with this thought about your relationship with your teachers: Teachers like students (and give them better grades) if they show genuine interest in the subject and the class. You don't have to be a teacher's pet or Nerd of the Month, but if you like what you're learning, show it.

If you've decided that you dislike chemistry almost as much as public speaking and major leg cramps, don't vent your anger and snide remarks to your teacher. He loves this stuff. He even goes to conventions where there are other chemistry teachers. He spends his weekends reading books like *50 Ways to Make Milkshakes with*

Hydrochloric Acid. Just endure. Do the best you can, and, best of all, go to him with honest questions about material that you don't understand. He's there to help you.

IT'S YOUR TURN

There. I'm done. You're just getting started.

Don't ever say again, "She gave me a C!" No, *she* didn't. *You* give yourself the grades you deserve, the grades you earn by either studying or goofing off. So what grade are you going to give yourself next time?

INDEX

Ron Fry's
HOW TO STUDY PROGRAM

Ron Fry's best-selling How to Study series is now completely updated and revised to help students meet the increasing demands of the school environment.

What makes the How to Study books so successful? According to Ron Fry, it's the concepts of time management and organization around which all six books in the series are built. "The keys," says Fry, "are to make the most of the time you have and enjoy what you're doing. It's easier than you think."

About the Author

Ron Fry is a nationally known spokesperson for the improvement of public education and an advocate for parents and students playing an active role in strengthening personal education programs. Aside from being the author of the vastly popular How to Study Series, Fry has edited or written more than 30 different titles — dynamic resources for optimum student success.

"Helpful for students of all ages from high school and up." – Small Press Book Review
"These are must-read guides every family should have in its library." – Library Journal

How to Study Series

• HOW TO STUDY, SIXTH EDITION
1-4018-8911-5, 2005
264 pp., 5 1/4" x 8 1/4", softcover,

• "ACE" ANY TEST, FIFTH EDITION
1-4018-8912-3, 2005
144 pp., 5 1/4" x 8 1/4", softcover

• GET ORGANIZED, THIRD EDITION
1-4018-8913-1, 2005
144 pp., 5 1/4" x 8 1/4", softcover

• IMPROVE YOUR MEMORY, FIFTH EDITION
1-4018-8914-X, 2005
144 pp., 5 1/4" x 8 1/4", softcover

• IMPROVE YOUR WRITING, FIFTH EDITION
1-4018-8916-6, 2005
168 pp., 5 1/4" x 8 1/4", softcover

• IMPROVE YOUR READING, FIFTH EDITION
1-4018-8915-8, 2005
144 pp., 5 1/4" x 8 1/4", softcover

Ordering Information

To Place an Order please call: (800) 842-3636 *or fax:* (859) 647-5963
Mailing address: Thomson Distribution Center, Attn: Order Fulfillment
                          10650 Toebben Drive, Independence, KY 41051

SOURCE CODE: CCCSNAH064